# Greenhouse Vegetable Gardening

Inger Palmstierna

# Greenhouse Vegetable Gardening

Expert Advice on
How to Grow
Vegetables, Herbs,
and Other Plants

Translated by
Gun Penhoat

Skyhorse Publishing

Skyhorse Publishing books may be purchased in bulk at special discounts for sales promotion, corporate gifts, fund-raising, or educational purposes. Special editions can also be created to specifications. For details, contact the Special Sales Department, Skyhorse Publishing, 307 West 36th Street, 11th Floor, New York, NY 10018 or info@skyhorsepublishing.com.

Skyhorse® and Skyhorse Publishing® are registered trademarks of Skyhorse Publishing, Inc.®, a Delaware corporation.

Visit our website at www.skyhorsepublishing.com.

10 9 8 7 6 5 4 3 2 1

Library of Congress Cataloging-in-Publication Data is available on file.

Cover design by Ingegärd Bodén
Cover photo credit by Inger Palmstierna

Print ISBN: 978-1-62914-739-0
Ebook ISBN: 978-1-62914-971-4

Printed in China

# CONTENTS

# Introduction

Many gardening enthusiasts take great pleasure in owning a greenhouse; they delight in its warmth, the scent of the earth and plants, the feeling of spring, the taste of summer, and the protection against blustery fall winds.

A gardener can plant, grow, and harvest cucumber and basil, as well as create a splendor of flowers in garden pots and flower beds. A greenhouse makes it possible to extend the growing season throughout the year, and to feel close to nature while remaining in sheltered comfort. A hobby greenhouse is seldom started as a money making venture, but the amount of plants and kilos of tomatoes that are often harvested within it make it profitable all the same.

The pleasure seeker can create a peaceful oasis with scents and greenery. A few well-chosen plants are enough to generate the right atmosphere, while still leaving enough space for an inviting seating arrangement.

No matter how we plan to enjoy our greenhouse, it needn't be expensive or cumbersome. We often unnecessarily over-complicate things when something simple fits the bill. Once we settle on how we'd like to use the greenhouse and furnish it accordingly, we can then make it both bountiful and easy to care for. There are many ways to create lush green happiness in the greenhouse—early snowdrops, pampered geraniums, sun-warmed tomatoes, shading vines, and fine plantings of summer flowers are only some of the myriad possibilities.

Those who already have a greenhouse will, in the first half of this book, get tips on additional plants you might consider growing. If the greenhouse isn't working in any of the ways you had hoped or anticipated, then you'll likely discover the cause in the book's second half, which deals with the hardware—the type of building, its size, shape, heat, and ventilation systems. Those who have not yet set up a greenhouse will glean useful information on what you need to take into account before you decide on a greenhouse structure.

The greenhouse is an environment that is warmer and lighter than our gardens and our homes. It allows the plants more time to grow, and gives us opportunities to cultivate more of them; it also requires more soil, water, fertilizer and care—an aspect of greenhouse gardening that might be somewhat tedious but nevertheless critical, and all the more fun and rewarding when successful. Together, the time and effort will turn your greenhouse into a wonderful, lush and flowering oasis, the gem of your garden.

Hven August 2006

*Inger Palmstierna*

# ACQUIRING A GREENHOUSE

A greenhouse is a fantastic asset. It offers many possibilities to any garden. It's ours to set up and use as we like, as a quiet corner to enjoy a cup of coffee or as a collection shed, or to give us an efficient boost in producing more vegetables by extending the growing season. You cannot, however, combine all those aspects into one single structure.

## Decisions and more decisions

Before you have the pleasure of actually owning a greenhouse, you'll have to decide how you wish to use it. This is probably the hardest part of selecting a greenhouse. If your priority is to have a comfortable outdoor room, you'll need to plan accordingly. On the other hand, if your goal is to increase your production of vegetables, you'll have to make sure that the plants get all the added space they require. Naturally, you can modify the plan from year to year if your needs or preferences change, but the construction and covering materials of the greenhouse will reflect its originally intended use.

If you want to have both a comfortable seating area for your coffee break and to grow tomatoes, you'll have to compromise. In Sweden, greenhouses that are smaller than 10 m² (107.5 ft²) don't require a permit if you follow all current building codes. This often means that the greenhouse space is limited, and therefore requires proper planning.

A greenhouse is comprised of a foundation, framework and roofing material; additional technical components such as ventilation, irrigation, and interior decoration should be selected and purchased at the same time as the greenhouse structure. If you're building a four-season greenhouse, you will have to plan for all the added elements before buying and laying down the foundation. A simpler heating system, such as a heating fan, can be added later.

## Reasonable cost

A very simple and practical way to get started is to buy a greenhouse kit. There is a multitude of greenhouse models available, in a wide range of sizes and styles, from Victorian gingerbread houses to ultra modern elegance, and wooden beauties. If you'd prefer to build your own custom greenhouse, there are many different ways to do that too. There is as much pleasure to be derived from a simple greenhouse built from old windows as there is from one designed to meet specific ideas, needs, wants, and environments.

The main components you should have in mind when buying a greenhouse are insulation and heating. Is the greenhouse going to be used throughout the entire year or only during part of it? If you're planning a four-season greenhouse and need to have permanent heating installed, your overall costs will be considerably larger than if you're satisfied with late spring, summer and early fall usage. While the price for heating in the north of Sweden is significant, in southern Sweden the cold doesn't linger quite as long, so the cost of heating tends to be lower.

*Previous page: There is room for both a comfortable seating area and lush greenery in a bigger greenhouse.*
*Right-hand page: Whether built from a kit or custom-made, there is grower's delight in both types of greenhouses.*

*Before you have the pleasure of actually owning a greenhouse, you'll have to decide how you wish to use it. This is probably the hardest part of selecting a greenhouse.*

Whether you're using your greenhouse for plantings or as an outdoor room, you will need to factor in the cost of heating. If you plan to use the greenhouse to overwinter plants, you'll save money on other storage solutions. Large olive trees, magnificent trumpet flowers, a geranium collection and other favorites thrive in a sunny and frost-free greenhouse, and heating costs can be offset by not purchasing new plants every spring.

The greenhouse's foundation needn't be the big production many imagine it to be. If the structure is not going to be heated during the winter months then the foundation doesn't take a lot of work. By all means dig, drain and lay down gravel, but it's generally not necessary for a smaller greenhouse. The exception is if you want a fully covered floor, which in smaller greenhouses can be set atop base rails placed directly on the ground, without having to sink in concrete post anchors. Such simply anchored greenhouses have weathered storms since 1988. Accidents can happen, but seldom have greenhouses toppled over due to an inadequate foundation.

If the greenhouse is going to be used as a four-season room, then the building requirements change and require advanced foundation work, along with different sets of costs. At this point you have to consider the structure an addition to your main house, and the expenses will be commensurate with what it would cost to add a room—one with glass walls.

*A larger greenhouse built from a kit and resting on base rails and slab.*

Acquiring a greenhouse is simple and the cost can be kept reasonable. There are many affordable options, so you don't need a complicated structure with an insulated foundation to enjoy it. It's a bit like with cars—driving a sporty coupe is fun, but you'll still make it to your destination at the wheel of a basic vehicle. The main thing is that it's functional and that it gets the job done.

Price range doesn't really affect the functionality of a greenhouse during the part of the year it's being used. However, the price of the greenhouse will influence how long during the year it can be used.

Don't let the high cost of a 'dream house' stop you from setting up a greenhouse. A cheaper greenhouse from a big box store will also give you a great deal of satisfaction. Just follow the recommendations in the accompanying leaflet and it can be adjusted and modified into a top-end model. My own greenhouses have been affordable options, and they've served me well during many years in different areas of Sweden, from central provinces like Uppland and Dalarna, all the way down to Skåne at the very south of the country. Gardening and spending time outdoors is a source of health and mental wellbeing; in a greenhouse—regardless of model or size—you can keep cultivating your health for the better part of the year.

# CULTIVATION

What gives the greenhouse its special atmosphere is its cultivation. Plants, water, and earth emit a wonderful smell and provide high humidity, but cultivation can be done in many different ways.

By deciding on which plants to grow and how much of the year to devote to them, it's possible to set up a practical and easily cared for greenhouse. Plan for what's most important to you: the pleasure of gardening, the seating for a leisurely coffee break, or for the economic benefits of cultivating vegetables and plants.

A common design is to make a narrow border along the length of the greenhouse where tall plants, such as tomatoes and cucumbers, can be set. You can install shelves for seeds and small plants along the opposite wall, or perhaps along the width of the greenhouse. To maximize the use of space even further, you can grow dill, lettuce, and basil in the soil between the tomato plants. Pepper and paprika planted in larger pots can line the path. You can even do all the cultivation in pots, the benefit being that plants are easy to move as needed, although they do need more care with watering and fertilizing.

If the greenhouse is a larger model, the short wall furthest away can be set aside for seating space for coffee breaks, in combination with a workbench. Very narrow shelves fastened to the house construction can hold a row of pots, which you can fill with favorites such as geraniums, fuchsia, and myrtle.

## How to grow

In a greenhouse you can cultivate plants and flowers in many different ways simultaneously.

You can raise plants in pots placed on the ground. You can also sow seeds directly into shallow boxes that contain soil. Dill, parsley, and lettuce grow well in boxes, too, if you harvest them as they grow.

It's also possible to grow plants and flowers directly in the ground in the greenhouse, in what are usually called beds. Larger plants such as tomatoes and cucumbers are typically grown in beds. First they're seeded in pots, and when the plants are big enough they're transferred to the growing area, either in the ground or in a bigger pot.

## What to grow

Most people grow tomatoes and cucumbers in their greenhouses but there are many other options, some of which are suggested in this book. To simplify cultivation and plant choice, plants that are treated the same way are all collected into growing groups. Regardless of whether it's a tomato or a cucumber, they grow very similarly, so instead of repeating the instructions for each plant, consider them applicable to all plants within the group. When it's time to increase the workload, make it simple on yourself by choosing plants within the same growing group—you'll have fewer details to keep in mind. As your joy in gardening increases, you can add other plant groups to your greenhouse.

*Carnation, one-year annual.*

*Nasturtium, a great choice for flower beds.*

*Tomatoes prefer the greenhouse.*

## Summer flowers for outdoor plantings (chap. 5)

Some plants don't reach the flowering stage before the first frost arrives, or flower extremely late if they aren't first started in a greenhouse. We like early flowers in beds and flowerpots. Petunias, Mexican marigolds, lobelia, and similar plants do flower even if direct seeded, but it won't be until late summer or early in the fall. If they can spend a month or two in the greenhouse beforehand, they will delight with flowers throughout summer. Even many bulbs and tubers risk freezing before flowering. Plants in hanging baskets and big planters are many times more beautiful if the plants are given a chance to fill out to their proper size in a greenhouse before they are hung in place.

## Wide bed sowing for bountiful flower beds (chap. 6)

It's very simple to pre-cultivate seedlings in the greenhouse for transplanting later into the ground and in flower beds. It's a very gratifying and easy way to grow flowers for bouquets and lush, colorful flower gardens. A greenhouse is the ideal place to get the most out of seeds and grow as many plants as possible. And if the seed is very expensive or rare, you don't want to sow it directly outside—in a greenhouse you don't run the risk of the seed rotting or birds and snails enjoying it as a snack. In a greenhouse, more seeds will probably germinate than in the ground outside.

## Growing vegetables in the greenhouse (chap. 7)

The most common greenhouse vegetables are the ones that don't have time to ripen outside—tomatoes, melons, eggplant, and hothouse cucumbers, for instance. In Sweden the summer season is simply too short, so you need to grow plants from seed to harvest in the greenhouse. During long hot summers they might grow in the ground, but this may not work reliably every time, and not in the country's northern parts. Depending on where you live, there will be other plants, like cape gooseberry (physalis), bell peppers and peppers, that also need to grow in a greenhouse to ensure that they will have time to ripen.

*Bean seedlings to transplant outside.*

*Tender lettuce for early harvesting.*

*Seedlings and early potatoes in a cold frame.*

## Vegetables to plant outside (chap. 8)

Vegetables are delicacies we enjoy in the summertime. Start growing vegetable seedlings in the greenhouse to transplant outside to ensure an earlier harvest. It also makes for less work weeding and thinning, even if the plants are very small when transplanted. Plants that require a lot of warmth to germinate, such as basil and pickle cucumbers, need to be started inside to ensure even germination and plenty of seedlings, and only then will they be ready to be transplanted outside. It's even good to start traditional herbs (like dill) in this manner to decrease the risk of fungal attacks.

## Early harvests in the greenhouse (chap. 9)

Greenhouse cultivation can bring a very early harvest of plants that you grow outside later on in the season. You can enjoy your own lettuce, delicate green onions and crisp radishes in early spring.

The early spring sun heats the greenhouse quicker than the ground outside, so if you grow seedlings in flats and then transplant them into the greenhouse soil, you will be harvesting those plants several weeks earlier than from the outside vegetable patch. Being able to harvest heat-loving herbs early adds that little something extra at mealtimes.

## Hotbeds and cold frames (chap. 10)

A hotbed is a good complement to the greenhouse. There is a centuries-old tradition of growing early vegetables—primeurs—in hotbeds. Starting in a greenhouse and transplanting into a hot or cold frame is an additional way to increase cultivation possibilities. Gherkins, squash and dill are examples of plants that need the greenhouse warmth to start growing before being transplanted to a cold frame. During the summer, melons like its warm soil. Also, beets, carrots and other primeurs can grow to an early harvest.

*Geraniums thrive in a greenhouse.*

*Pansies can be made to bloom early.*

*Spring flowering nectarine in the greenhouse.*

## A greenhouse in flower year-round (chap. 11)

It's necessary to mix different kinds of plants in the greenhouse if it is to become a green oasis year-round. Small hardy trees like peach, apricot and nectarine are in bloom so early in the year their flowers will freeze if they're kept outside. These can be grown in pots or directly in the ground. A mature grapevine will give summer shade and bunches of sweet grapes. Annuals, perennial Mediterranean plants and traditional plants such as roses contribute to the beauty.

Plants that are not hardy and need to be kept cool and in proper light during the winter will flourish in the greenhouse during the summer. These are plants like camellia, citrus, and olive trees, bay leaf, rosemary, and myrtle that cannot be kept in homes. Many plants, among them bougainvillea and passion flower need a warmer climate in order to develop and flower.

## Overwintering plants in a greenhouse (chap. 12)

The greenhouse can be used to overwinter (hibernate) less hardy species—which ones depend on where you live. Plants grown in pots year-round are more cold sensitive. Thus, a greenhouse environment is beneficial for them, too.

## Spring flowers, bulbs, and perennials (chap. 13)

To produce early blooms outside, it's possible to plant bulbs in a pot and let it overwinter in the greenhouse, thus forcing an earlier flowering. Even other spring flowers like primulas and pansies can be sown in the fall, transplanted into a pot, overwintered, and then forced into an extra-early flowering. If you want to grow your own perennials, sow them during the summer and let them overwinter in the greenhouse before transplanting them the following year. This way

you'll succeed in growing new gems and difficult plants that do not like cold or wet winters.

## Houseplants—cuttings and seeds (chap. 14)

Houseplants or indoor plants, which we keep inside our homes, flourish in a greenhouse. If you want to take cuttings or plant seeds from houseplants, the greenhouse is the right place to do it. Treasured favorites like geraniums grow more handsomely in a greenhouse, and many other plants benefit from a rejuvenating cure in the greenhouse's light and airy atmosphere.

It's even possible to multiply plants such as potentilla (cinquefoil), roses, and other ornamental shrubs yourself. Plants prefer an area that's a little warmer and more protected while they're developing roots, even though these plants are meant to be outside year-round.

# GREEN OR BROWN THUMB GARDENER?

Growing plants is an endeavor that is both simple and complex. There's nothing easier than pushing a seed into the soil, which then grows into a plant. If everything goes as planned, that's all it takes. There is, however, more to cultivating plants that are grown specifically for their blooms.

While all plants need light, water, nutrients and warmth to grow, they don't all require the same amount of all of these elements. Our most common weeds germinate quickly and manage well on their own. A tomato germinates easily, while a cucumber needs more warmth to grow. When a gardener ensures that the plants get what they need to thrive, their cultivation becomes simpler, requires less work and yields better harvests, whether they're flowers or fruit. And it's easier to treat them right if we understand how plants grow.

A seed needs moisture to germinate. It's like a packet of dried food, in that it needs water to become rehydrated—the seed needs to be enveloped by humid soil so it can swell and grow. The soil also has to be free of weeds and disease, and needs to be devoid of nutrients. This kind of soil is called potting soil; it's widely available and can be purchased in bags. It's important to use potting soil here, as neither planting, compost nor topsoil work very well. Common planting soil contains too many nutrients, and topsoil harbors weed seeds that will compete with the sown seeds.

## Soil

When the seed has germinated, it's then placed in its own pot with nutrient-rich soil. Please note that even store-bought plants need to be potted up into bigger receptacles with nutrient-rich soil. When selecting your soil (sometimes sold as plant soil, flower soil, or garden soil), do not opt for the cheapest brand available, as its price usually reflects the quality and quantity of nutrients in the soil. If you buy the cheap soil, you will end up having to buy supplemental nutrients to amend it. And you need to ensure that the soil you buy is weed- and disease-free.

It's fine to use compost or garden soil when you pot up your plant—simply mix equal amounts of compost and garden soil for optimum results. This soil is not free of weeds, however, and you will have to pull them as they appear. If you have many big pots you'll need a lot of soil, so adding garden soil to your store-bought soil will make it go further. Commercial soil contains mostly peat which, when mixed with a half-and-half mix of garden soil and compost, will become slightly sturdier and won't dry into a hard lump.

*Early spring in the greenhouse. Seedlings to transplant—both flowers and vegetables. Trays of plants to be grown in the greenhouse. Over-wintered nectarines and geraniums in full bloom. Artichokes that were planted in January and sprouting-seed potatoes. All need light, water, nutrients, and good soil.*

## Compost

Most plants grow well in regular planting soil. When you sow your seeds, use the same soil for all the seeds. Do not use compost for seeds, or for any plants that require acidity. Even compost from decayed oak leaves will not produce acidic compost, as nature tends to interfere. Compost that is amended with chicken manure for extra nitrogen, however, is excellent for larger plants and for general soil nutrient balance. Compost is also ideal because it contains naturally occurring beneficial bacteria and insects that do not come in commercial soil.

Compost's high content of microbial populations, worms and insects makes it naturally pest-resistant, and even helps plants absorb nutrients. All fungi and bacteria in compost and well-balanced soil work in symbiosis with the plants' root systems, so using soil amended with compost is a shortcut to a healthy and easy-to-care-for garden.

## Nutrient storehouse

Plants can be grown in many ways. They can be raised in pots, either large or small, depending on the final size of the plant. They can also be planted in the ground soil of the greenhouse. It's even possible to set them directly into the purchased bags of soil, or grow them out of sand and grass clippings. While all these different methods have their pros and cons, the common factor is that they will at some point run out of nutrients during the growing season, so the soil will need to be enriched regularly.

## Someone to lean on

The soil isn't just a storehouse for nutrients and water—the plants also need it for support. The roots anchor the plants in the soil so they don't topple over in a strong wind or buckle under their own weight. That's why the soil needs to go deep. A 10 cm (4") layer of soil per square meter area is not the same as growing something at a depth of 30 cm (12") in the same patch of earth, so it's preferable that the plant be placed in a pot or in a hole that's at least 30 cm (12") deep. The deeper you set it, the more stable the plant, and the more even the distribution of nutrients and water. You won't have to water and fertilize as frequently, and the earth does not get as warm. (You want the soil to be warm in springtime, but in summer it can often heat up to the point of being detrimental to growth.) Ground soil does not heat up as much as potting soil in a container.

## Airy and loose

For plant roots to be able to draw up water and nutrients from their environment, the soil needs to be loose. First, roots need air to breathe, or else they will slowly but steadily suffocate. Second, soil has to be loose in order to allow the roots to grow and thrive. The roots push through the soil while growing, and are unable to do so if the soil is too compacted, thus preventing them from reaching further to get additional water and nutrients.

The roots also have to spread unrestricted in the soil; a stone, cement paver or a patch of hard compacted earth will stop them. Driving a heavy wheelbarrow or repeatedly walking on the soil will tamp down and compact the earth, so it's advisable to never walk or kneel directly in the beds, cold frames or raised beds. This way you also avoid the added workload of re-digging and changing out the compacted earth.

## Growing directly in the ground

Growing plants directly in the ground is both simple and traditional. The soil is a storehouse of water and nutrients where the roots have plenty of room to thrive, and can reach and reap the benefits of deeper sources of water and nutrients. Consequently, careful watering of the roots and plants is not essential, and it's also easier to train plants to grow vertically (see chapter 7, page 62).

Avoid raising the same plants in the same soil year after year, as doing so can attract pests that feed on and destroy the plants early in the spring. The disadvantage to this method is that you have to add new soil or amend the existing ground soil each spring. One way to avoid this drudgery is to mix plenty of compost into the beds before starting to plant, as compost helps keep soil healthy and full of nutrients. Another option is to rotate the placement of plants, with cucumbers on one side and tomatoes

*The in-ground bed soil and compost is amended and covered with store-bought planting soil—an effective way to prevent weeds.*

on the other one year, and switching them around the following year, for example.

When you work the ground in the greenhouse for the first time, it should be dug to a depth of 25 to 30 cm (10 to 12 inches) in order to loosen the earth and make it crumbly. It's OK to use a garden fork for this task. An 20 cm (8-inch-high) layer of compost is then laid on top and methodically worked into the ground. This leaves the soil piled quite high above the rest of the ground, so you can add edging made out of wood planks or stones to limit or prevent soil erosion. The soil level will sink and become level with the surrounding ground as the plants gradually absorb nutrients.

Each batch of spent soil should be removed and replaced with store-bought planting soil or compost. If you don't want to change all of the soil each spring, you will have to amend it with plenty of compost to keep it healthy. Old soil can be used in many other ways in the garden.

## Growing in containers

A more flexible option than growing plants in the ground is to grow them in containers. Big pots are filled with soil and plants—the soil can be store-bought planting soil that is mixed with compost, as well as topsoil, if you so wish. It's easy to switch growing mediums every year to give plants a healthy and disease-free environment. And if a pest or disease happens to strike one container, it's unlikely to spread to the others. It's also a foolproof way to accommodate plants that need special soils or require an especially large amount of nutrients, since it's possible to have different soils in the different pots.

The drawback to this is that a container's soil tends to warm up and dry out more quickly than on the ground, so you'll have to keep a watchful eye and provide extra water, and boost nutrition as needed. Generally, larger containers grow healthier plants—a 10-liter (2 1/2 gallon) bucket is almost too small for

*Plants in the ground and in big containers. The plants in pots need more frequent watering than the plants in the ground bed.*

*Grow directly in bags of planting soil.*

The inconvenience with this method is that the soil's temperature rises quickly (like for potted plants) so it's necessary to be extra vigilant about watering. The layer of soil is shallow and doesn't provide much stability for the plant, so it has a tendency to become lanky. And if there's a paved or cemented area underneath the bags, the plants will be especially prone to drying out, as the roots will be unable to reach into the cooler ground below.

## Growing in sand and grass clippings

Growing plants in sand with grass clippings is a method that has piqued the interest of many. Sand contains no nutrients, but keeps its shape and is easily watered. The nourishment for the plant is supplied by fresh grass clippings, which are deposited onto the sand's surface. The nutrients in the clippings are quickly broken down (as in surface composting) and dissolve in the sand's water, and in this manner become accessible to the plants. While this method is highly successful, the harvest is neither better nor worse than in-ground planting.

The inconvenience here is that grass clippings must be added in a thin layer once a week. It also takes a while for the clippings' decomposition process to begin, so it's necessary to add manure initially. You also have to collect sand for the plant, and sand is heavy. Grass clippings are always useful somewhere in the garden.

Fresh grass clippings can be used to mulch around roses, vegetables and summer flowering plants. Just layer the clippings 0.5 to 1 cm (¼ to ½ inches) thick several times over the first half of the summer. If you choose to leave finely chopped clippings on the lawn they will soon break down into nourishment for the lawn itself. If you add the clippings to the compost pile they will decompose quickly, so make sure the clippings are properly mixed into the composting material; if not, they will form into a dry, foul-smelling layer on top of the pile.

a tomato or cucumber plant. Also, stay away from dark colored containers and pots, as they tend to absorb heat, and this in turn may overwhelm and burn your plants, especially in summer. Pots may be moved around the greenhouse, but training large plants in this way can become cumbersome.

Boxed beds are a variation of growing plants in pots. Boxes built with untreated lumber can be easily set up to suit the greenhouse's plan. As with containers, the soil in a planting box should be changed each year. If the box has no foundation, the plant roots can grow into the ground soil. Raised beds are a great option if lower back issues are a concern; they also make gardening accessible to those who use a wheelchair, as it's easier to reach and care for the plants.

## Growing plants in a bag

A growing method wedged somewhere between using containers and the ground is to grow plants directly in a bag. A 55- to 65-quart sack filled with good plant soil is laid flat on the ground (the ground underneath the bag should be porous, so avoid setting it on cement or asphalt).

Cut a few X's on the underside of the bag—the side that rests on the ground—this is where the excess water will drain. In time, the plant roots will grow through the bag and into the ground, which allows them to benefit from the water and nutrients found in the ground below the bag. Cut one or two holes on the surface of the bag and insert one plant into each hole. You can place rows of bags in the greenhouse. In the fall, simply remove the bags and empty their contents into your vegetable garden, the compost heap or flower beds; buy new bags of soil in the spring.

## Nutrients

All plants need regularly added nutrients, but greenhouse plants that grow more abundant and faster than in-ground garden plants require an especially large amount of fertilizer. You can amend the soil, as well as purchase soil that is extra rich in nutrients. However, this food lasts only about three to five weeks, after which it becomes necessary to add more supplements. You can also water plants with liquid fertilizer—add it to the soil or install an automatic irrigation system complete with liquid nutrients.

*A garden's goldmine is its compost pile. With its contents you can fill all the big garden pots and planters; in the spring it helps amend the beds in the greenhouse with nutrient-rich top dressing.*

## Organic and manufactured fertilizers

Fertilizers are available in either manufactured or organic formulations. In Sweden, some manufactured, also called commercial, fertilizers go by the names of EnPeKå, Blåkorn and TGVäx Upp. Organic fertilizer can be cow manure, chicken manure, or a mixture of several natural by-products such as blood meal and bone meal. There is even organic fertilizer that has been amended with manufactured fertilizer. Whichever fertilizer you decide to use can be found in both solid and liquid forms. Solid fertilizers are worked into the soil, whereas liquid versions are diluted and then watered in. For fertilizer to be ready to use by the plants, it has to be incorporated into the soil's moisture. Roots draw up the water containing small concentrations of nutrients from the manure and soil, making it important to water after the addition of manure to the soil.

The inherent convenience of commercial fertilizer is that it dissolves in water and is available to the plants right away. Its downside is that any amount of fertilizer that is not taken up by the plants runs into the ground and subsoil, along with the irrigation water; too much fertilizer leached into the ground water increases the nitrogen content of our lakes and waterways, which in turn causes a proliferation of algae that is detrimental to the environment.

Organic fertilizer, on the other hand, needs to break down in the soil before the plants can make use of it. This takes a bit more time and can delay the availability of nutrients to the plant, which might be a problem. The flip side is that the breakdown of this type of fertilizer is sustained as long as the soil temperature remains at or above 5°C (41°F), which means that there will always be some nutrients available to the plants, which is healthy. Organic fertilizer is also beneficial to the soil fauna that's involved in breaking down the nutrients in the soil, and that also keeps the soil loose, airy, and porous. Earthworms, as well as useful bacteria and fungi that work in symbiosis with plant roots, much prefer soil nourished with organic fertilizer to one boosted by commercial fertilizer.

## All-day snacking

Plants grow best when they're given an even, steady supply of nutrients; a small but constant release means that they'll always have food when they need it. Plants don't absorb more nutrients than they need at any given time, even when there is a surplus (there are some notable exceptions, one of them being nitrogen). By contrast, administering large amounts of fertilizer in fewer doses is seldom beneficial to plants—it's not a good idea to fertilize them heavily and then leave them over long spells between feedings. Once nutrients are dissolved, plants absorb whatever they need immediately, and the excess nutrients will seep into the ground—and groundwater—and be lost to the plant. Since plants only ever eat what they need at any given moment, they will lack nutrients until the next time you feed them. Fertilizing plants in this manner will result in sparse growth, lack of blooms and skimpy harvests, while creating more harmful chemical run-offs in our waterways.

## Food every time

Among the many liquid fertilizers available on the market, some feature attachments that plug directly into a garden-hose spray nozzle for easy and convenient fertilizing. This is not a method that I recommend, however, since spray nozzles are not at all suitable for watering plants. A far better and practical feeding option is to mix liquid fertilizer and water in a drip irrigation system, type Hydromat, so that plants receive a continuous, slow release of nutrients.

Another way is to add slow-release fertilizer pellets to the soil. They look like tiny dots and are often found in good quality, store-bought fertilizers. The fertilizer itself is enclosed in the pellets, and is gradually released as the pellets' outer shells disintegrate over time. The amount of nutrients released from the pellets depends on the warmth and humidity of the growing medium—the warmer and more humid the soil is, the more nutrients are released within it. Plants tend to grow more quickly when the environment is warm and humid, and the quicker plants grow, the more food they require to avoid becoming undernourished.

Yet another efficient fertilizing method is to use a watering can to water the plants with water mixed with soluble fertilizer. Swedish trials have shown that most plants thrive and grow vigorously when given the Swedish plant food equivalent to Miracle-Gro, 'Blomstra', in amounts of 1 ml per liter (1 quart) of water, per watering. Big plants need more water and more food compared to smaller plants; plants grown in warmer environments will grow faster and therefore also require more water and fertilizer.

All small pots with seedlings for transplanting, as well as hanging baskets, summer bulbs, corms, rhizomes, and other plants cultivated in the greenhouse should be irrigated with liquid fertilizer, since the potting soil contains hardly any nutrients at all. Peat pellets with vegetable seedlings also thrive when fed regularly, once the seed has sprouted and the first couple of leaves appear. Summer flowers in planters, window box arrangements, and potted houseplants also flourish when administered a mix of water and Blomstra. (It's the perfect blend to use on bushes, flower beds and vegetable patches, too, but those garden spaces require a much larger amount of the mix). To an average-sized three-gallon watering can, add two teaspoons of Blomstra—this would be about 10 ml of liquid fertilizer per can of water.

*A watering can containing a weak fertilizer solution is a good option for watering plants. Fill the can and let its contents rise to the ambient temperature of the greenhouse.*

## The right plant food

Plants require nutrients in order to grow and flower; if you are stingy with food they will not thrive. Pour on too much fertilizer, however, and you may also end up with undesirable results. Nitrogen (chemical symbol N) is a nutrient that plants readily gobble up, and when they absorb more than they need they grow huge, resulting in tall, foliage-heavy plants that give little fruit or blooms. Potatoes end up large, watery and flat tasting; tomatoes are tasteless, and hot peppers lack heat. So instead of making a hit and miss mixture of one's own, it's better to buy a ready-made blend that contains perfectly balanced nutrients - the Swedish Blomstra and Chrysan are good examples of such products. If you opt for other brands, be sure the nitrogen (N) content does not exceed 5% to 10%. The mix should also contain micronutrients. The fertilizer feeds containing all the nutrients that plants need are usually referred to as complete fertilizers. A good fertilizer is not expensive, but a really cheap product is definitely a false economy, as it will lack important nutrients—and plants need around twenty different nutrients such as iron, manganese, and calcium in order to grow. Those nutrients must also be in a form that plants can easily absorb. If the label only says NPK (Nitrogen Phosphorus Potassium) with no further detail in the fine print, the product will most likely be missing the rest of the necessary nutrients.

## Special needs

Different soils contain different nutrients. Nearly all commercially available bagged soil is made from peat moss. Peat moss is harvested in peat bogs and is acidic, weed free, loose, and contains no nutrients. Starting off with this base makes it easier to mix it to the desired final composition, as all plants don't need the same amounts and types of nutrients—some want more of this and others prefer more of that; some plants even require special fertilizer and special soil. Nevertheless, most plants will thrive in limed, alkaline, and fertilized soil.

Plants that don't do well in alkaline soil need acidic soil instead, also called rhododendron soil. For example, rhododendron, camellia and labruscana grapes (concord and niagara) need acidic soil and fertilizer. These plants have great difficulty absorbing nutrients like iron if they are planted in the wrong soil—their growth is stunted and their leaves turn yellow. Citrus soil is good for citrus plants, as it contains quite a bit of clay and is slightly heavier than normal alkaline planting soil while being also slightly acidic (citrus plants are often plagued by yellowing leaves if they're planted in regular planting soil). It's good to provide roses with their own special soil, but it's not necessary. The special soil contains a fair bit of clay, which roses seem to thrive in.

Geranium soil contains an extra large amount of fertilizer, both in slow-release and in readily available forms, which makes nutrients available to plants over a long period of time. This steady source of nutrients is necessary because geraniums need a lot of food to flower profusely. Potted clematis also like geranium soil, as large-bloom clematis require lots of food to blossom abundantly.

Planting soil is necessary for sowing in pots and flower beds. In Sweden, a good choice would be 50-liter (13 1/2 gallon) sacks of Hasselfors S-soil (lightly fertilized, loose, porous soil containing perlite). Leftover soil can always be used to start growing potatoes from seed.

Potted summer flowers and hanging baskets demand a special U-soil (containing both slow and quick release nutrition) or some other good quality soil containing slow-release fertilizer. Geranium soil is suitable here, too.

Economy-priced soil can be used to amend flower beds and vegetable patches. If it's mixed half and half with garden soil and some added manure, it can be used for planting perennials in the ground; it cannot be used in pots, containers, hanging baskets, or window boxes, since these vessels require more nutrient-rich growth media due to their smaller size. Even the best of soil, however, does not hold enough nutrition to last a geranium or tomato plant through the summer (were that the case, it would be so potent as to become poisonous to the plant). This is why it's necessary to irrigate the plant with fertilized water after one month or in late summer, depending on plant type and weather conditions.

In addition to special soils and fertilizers, there are also special products aimed at intensifying or lowering the acidity of soils. An example of one such product available in Sweden is 'Färga mig blä' ('Color me blue') which is used to acidify soil in order to force blue blooms on hydrangeas instead of the more common pink blooms, which are typical of flowers planted in a regular alkaline soil.

*Top: Geranium soil is extra rich in nutrients.*
*Middle: Rose soil contains clay.*
*Bottom: Citrus soil is slightly acidic.*

# PLANTING, PRE-CULTIVATION, POTTING UP

Aside from being a lot of fun, it's probably also more economical to use a greenhouse for planting and pre-cultivation. Perennials, annuals, and vegetables can be sown and pre-cultivated in the greenhouse.

*The text on the seed packet contains important information, so read it carefully before opening it.*

The great advantage of a greenhouse is that you can start your plants from seed. Pre-cultivation is another term for starting plants from seed; in gardening terminology, "to cultivate" means "to grow." Seed starting brings about earlier harvest and blooming for plants in window boxes, pots, and hanging baskets. You can then go on to fill your garden beds and borders with vegetables and flowers.

The time to start your seeds depends not only on what kind of plants you'd like to grow; it also hinges on how long the seedlings need to grow, as well as on how big a hurry you are in to see results. If you wish for plants similar to those sold at garden centers, you need to count on seeding and then potting them up once or twice. If you want a quick and simple way to transplant many plants to flower beds, wide sowing in flats is a good way to go.

## Seeds

You can sow seeds very early, from late winter into spring. You don't need to provide a lot of light during germination, as the flats can stay anywhere it's sufficiently warm. As soon as the seeds have germinated, however, the addition of a growth light becomes necessary. If you sow early, you need to move the germinated seeds into a heated greenhouse, or keep them in your home, but make sure to provide extra growth light.

The simplest way is to start seeds in your home if you don't have a properly heated greenhouse—it's easier to keep an eye on the seedlings. Once the seedlings start to grow, you then move them into a light-filled greenhouse. The later in spring you start the seeds, the simpler this process will be. It gets both warmer and lighter every week, which is better for both seedlings and plants. When the greenhouse starts to warm up you can place the seedlings in there unless the temperature dips during the night (the temperature needs to hold steady around 10°C (50°F) during the night).

Seed trays don't take up a lot of space, so a greenhouse isn't really necessary to keep them. You can place the trays close together on a kitchen bench and provide direct light from above—see suggestion for lighting on page 33. However, when it's time to transplant or pot up the seedlings after a few weeks, this space will eventually become overcrowded and will not provide enough light—that's when it is time to move into the greenhouse. If it's still too cold at night, you can use a fan heater to warm up the space. You can also place the plants and seedlings in an insulated growing cabinet in the greenhouse (a cabinet doesn't require as much energy to keep warm as a whole greenhouse). Another solution is to buy a small hot-bed: they radiate heat from the bottom up, which is good for the seedlings' growth; you can easily add a growth light to this bed when needed.

# How to's—Sowing

◆ Buy the appropriate seed starting mixture. These mixes are sold in well-stocked nurseries and garden centers, and usually contain perlite—small white pellets that keep the soil porous and damp.

• Read the instructions on the seed packets. Some seeds, not all, need to be covered.

• Sow in shallow containers, or flats, that have been filled with the seed-starting blend. Pour in some of the mixture, then tamp it down lightly so that it's somewhat compacted. Press more firmly in the corners where the soil has a tendency to sink. You can use a tamping board with a handle to pat down the soil.

• Place the container or flat on a level surface and sift over a final thin layer of soil. The easiest way to do this is to use a soil sieve or a larger kitchen sieve.

◆ Sprinkle seeds sparsely over the soil surface. You can seed double the amount of plants you wish to grow, but not more. If you sow too many seeds, the container will become overcrowded with spindly seedlings having to struggle under the growth light or on the windowsill. Better to grow ten healthy seedlings than twenty puny ones.

• Sieve a thin soil covering over the seeds. The thickness of the covering will depend on the seed packet instructions, and can range from one millimeter (0.04") for small seeds, to one centimeter (0.40") for large seeds.

◆ Mist the surface of a pot *without drainage hole*, using a misting bottle. A watering can might set the seeds floating around the surface of the soil and then they'll collect in a clump. The seedlings become too crowded and will grow thin and lanky. The roots grow together and tear apart when it's time to separate the seedlings for transplanting.

• A pot *with drainage hole* should never be watered from the top down, but should be placed in a water-filled tray instead. The sowing mixture soaks up the water from the bottom until the surface is moist.

◆ Place the seed containers in a mini greenhouse system or on trays. Seeds that are not covered with soil must be kept in a mini greenhouse or be covered by glass, plastic or similar material in order to keep the soil surface damp so the seeds can germinate.

• Keep the mini greenhouse at normal room temperature, preferably above a radiator so it's warmed from below.

*Top: Sieve the top layer of soil when sowing small seeds.*
*Middle: Large seeds can be planted one by one in the flat.*
*Bottom: Mini greenhouses with lids are good for seed starting, but use caution when watering.*

*Above: Seed-sowing at different stages. Not all seeds are started at the same time. Some, like geraniums are sown in January; most others in March-April. Below: Marigolds ready for potting up.*

◆ As soon as plants emerge, the mini greenhouse needs to be moved into the light, and also to where it's cooler. Depending on the time of year, the light in the windowsill might suffice. If not, it'll be necessary to hang cool-white fluorescent bulbs for extra light above the plantings.

• Check the plantings every day. Pour or wipe off condensation from the mini greenhouse, plastic bag or glass cover. Mold will grow if water is allowed to drip down onto the plantings.

• You can carefully ventilate the plantings once they're green. Some mini greenhouses have a small vent in the roof that can be opened. If not, lodge something like a matchstick between the cover and the box so air can circulate. You can reduce condensation in this way and reduce the risk of the plant developing rot.

• The plantings might dry out if it's a sunny day. Water, whenever possible, from below.

31

*Direct-seeded large seeds (e.g., cucumber), in pots.*

*Direct-seeded small seeds (e.g., Lobelia), in plant ready pots.*

## Planting in pots

The size of small pots is established by measuring the diameter in centimeters; the size of larger pots is read in liters (quarts). A round pot is measured straight across the top; the most common sizes are between 7 to 20 centimeters (2 3/4" to 8"). Smaller sizes are usually square— approximately 5 x 5 cm (2" x 2") or 8 x 8 cm (3" x 3"). The pots can, of course, vary in depth: a 3" x 3" pot can be either shallow or deep. Bigger pots are measured in liters (quarts) and can range from 1 to 1.5 liters (1 to 1.5 quarts) to 5 liters (5 quarts) or larger.

When it comes to purchasing plants, the size of the pot is directly related to the price. A plant in a 2" x 2" pot is smaller than a plant in an 8" x 8" pot, and thus the former is cheaper than the latter, as it's possible to produce more plants per square foot when sowing. The smaller plant occupies less space when transported and less soil is needed for its wellbeing. A grower will often fit a plant into the smallest pot he can get away with to remain competitive in the marketplace. For this reason, a store-bought pot's size isn't an adequate reference to go by when choosing your own pot to grow your plant in. Do plant and grow plants in the biggest pots you can afford to make them sturdy and healthy. What you should avoid doing, however, is transplanting a small seedling directly from the seed tray into a much larger container, because it will then expend its energy growing mostly roots, and not very much above ground.

Summer flowers come in 6-section trays called 6-packs, separation-less growing boxes, and specialty pots. By all means save them and reuse them for your own sowing and plantings, but remember that the plants are very tightly spaced. This works fine for the nursery worker who can

provide extra growth light and heating, but can be a bit crowded for the hobby greenhouse. As plants grow, it's customary to separate the pots and to space them out in order to give the plants room to develop evenly all around. This is impossible if they're clustered, egg-carton style, in 6-packs.

## Few and large seeds

Big seeds from beans, pumpkins, cucumbers and melons are sown singly in their own individual pots. They are covered with at least 1/2" of soil and don't need a glass or plastic cover or to stay in a mini greenhouse, as they already are covered by the soil. They do need plenty of warmth to germinate, however, and ought to be placed on a tray above a radiator. The seeds are sown in large pots 7 to 8 cm (about 2 3/4" to 3") in diameter, and they don't like having their roots disturbed. When they are large enough to be transplanted, you need to be extra careful: lift the whole plant out of the pot, along with the soil and roots in one big clump. The clump is then placed into its new, bigger, 14 to 15 cm (5 1/2" to 6") pot, without disturbing the roots. Fill up the pot all around the clump with new soil.

## Many small seeds

Some seeds are sown a few at a time in a small pot and are not transplanted into another pot. When sowing really small seeds, such as Lobelia, it's tricky to see how closely they are sown. Lobelia should be sown 5 to 8 seeds per 5 x 5 cm (2" x 2") pot. One way to sow these types of seeds is to mix them with fine-grain aquarium sand in a bowl and then pat it down. The sand makes it easier to spot what is sown, ensuring that there are not too many seeds in each pot.

*Many small seedlings waiting to be potted up.*

Sowing small seeds is a bit of an art form, and there are many different ways to do it. Among these are: placing the sand-mix on the edge of a knife; using a pepper shaker; dabbing with a pencil or fingertip, etc.

Summer geraniums have extremely small seeds. They are sold as pelletized seeds, which means they have been encased in clay. The seeds look like pinhead-sized clay balls, which can be sown one by one. Pelletizing is a costly treatment that is only done to high-quality seeds, but it is well worth the expense for some seeds. Pelletized seeds need extra high moisture to germinate; the clay cover is softened by the dampness and splits open when the seedling emerges.

## Seed viability and germination time

Seeds have different germination times, and even variations in seed viability; this information can be found on the seed packet. If the seed has a low germination rate, you'll sow a bit closer together. Don't be alarmed if growth takes several weeks to appear, as some seeds are more temperamental than others—but this should be no reason to give up. It shouldn't be necessary to water the seeds before some green appears, but that too can vary. The sown surface should be damp. If the seeds have long germination times the surface might dry up before the seeds have time to grow. Regardless, never water directly on the sown surface, as the seeds can rot if the conditions are too humid and too crowded.

## Growth light

Early seeding requires light for sustained growth. There is a big difference between the quality of daylight in February and that of April. Seeds sown later in the season can catch up with seeds sown earlier, as the earlier seeds have had less light to work with. January, February, and March until the Spring Equinox are the darker months of the year where artificial light is of great assistance. It's easy to make a temporary light source by hanging fluorescent light tubes above the seeded containers. If you need to light more than seedlings—perhaps you have camellias in bloom in the greenhouse—then you need a more permanent lighting solution, which is shown on page 174.

Fluorescent cold white tubes are, however, perfectly adequate for the plantings inside your house. They are long and narrow and fit over a window bench or similar structure. The tubes should hang approximately 25 to 30 cm (10" to 12") above the plants. Better yet if you can lower and raise the lights. One way to do this is to attach the light with screws to a movable shelf structure; the desired height of the light source can then be found by raising or lowering the shelf. Saw horses that can be lowered and raised will also work. If the light fixture is not movable, however, the sown flats can be moved up or down. Simply place them onto boxes of a variety of heights to achieve the best distance.

There's an advantage to keeping the sown flats on trays in order to limit water spillage. There are also special seed boxes with holes in the bottom; two can fit together on a larger, watertight tray. Or they can be placed in a mini greenhouse that always has a watertight base. A light fixture of 2W x 11W, or 2W x 18W, is enough for many seedlings if you practice interval planting and use windowsills. Keep the growth lights on twelve to fourteen hours per day during the light period, in order to mimic true daylight. Remove the protective hood from the fluorescent tubes as it only steals light away from the seedlings, and perhaps add a timer for convenience as well as energy savings.

## Right temperature

Once the seedlings have emerged, they will spend a short time growing in the seed box. Most plants thrive in temperatures held around 16°C to 18°C (61°F to 64.5°F). How long they stay in the seed box depends on the type of plant, but anywhere between one to five weeks is typical. The seedling in the box needs to grow two slightly rounded leaves—the cotyledons—that come from the seed. Then a second pair of leaves arrives, which are the first set of true leaves characteristic of the plant. At this point it's time to transplant, (also called potting up or potting on) the seedling into another container. Most, but not all, plants have two cotyledons. Plants from bulbs, such as lilies and grasses, have one leaf that is long and narrow like a blade of grass.

# How to's—Potting up

Fill clean pots with planting mix before starting to pot up. The containers must be thoroughly scoured of all old planting mix that could harbor disease or pests from prior years. The soil should be a commercial, good quality planting mix. Pour this mix up to the pot's rim and tap it down so the pot is half full, then pour in more soil to fill it up again to the rim. The soil should be firm but not hard, which could hinder the roots' development. It should allow the seedling and soil to be removed intact from the pot once it's time to plant out. After watering, the soil will shrink a little, so it will not quite reach the rim. Place the pots on a level surface— preferably on plastic trays—to make them easy to move.

◆ Loosen the seedlings in the seed tray. Soggy or dry soil is a no-no. Soil that is slightly damp is best, so if it's dry, water and hold off on the transplanting until the following day. Loosen the soil from below, and never pull on the seedling itself. Gently push your fingers, a frying spatula or a wide wooden plant marker under the soil along the bottom of the pot/tray (see top picture). Lift a whole clump of seedlings and soil and set it beside the tray.

◆ Carefully separate the plants by pulling the soil—not the plants—apart, from the middle and out. See center picture. The plants will separate sideways, free of the soil clump.

◆ Take hold of the seedling, not by the stem but by one of the cotyledons. Lift the seedling with your left hand if you're right-handed. Make a deep hole in the new container's soil with your right hand. Use a finger, a pencil or a special potting pin (poke) and make a hole all the way to the bottom of the container and place the plant roots in the hole. With the right hand tuck some soil around the seedling. When the seedling is nestled in the hole, use left and right fingers to push the soil so there is proper contact between soil and plant roots. See top picture, next page.

◆ The seedling is usually planted deeper than when it was sown in the seed tray to prevent it from becoming tall and leggy. All the roots and part of the stem are placed within the planting hole, and it's important to tuck the soil snuggly around the roots so there is proper contact. If the hole is not deep enough, or if the roots are very long, trim them a little; never coil the roots so they are doubled up in the bottom of the container—it's far better to trim the roots to shorter length. That's why it's best to sow seeds in shallow trays or pots: it will encourage shorter roots.

◆ Make sure to label your seedlings, as many tend to look alike.

◆ Place the new plantings on a tray and let them draw water from below.

## Mini greenhouses

If you have several mini greenhouses, the newly potted-up plants can stay there for a few days until they've settled in their new containers. Place them in as much light as possible but in a slightly cooler temperature than before—approximately 15°C to 16°C (59°F to 61°F). The warmer the environment, the taller and leggier the plants will become. Room temperature around 22°C to 24°C (71.6°F to 75°F) is too warm for the plants. At this point you can also put them in a greenhouse, glass-walled balcony or deck, as long as it doesn't get too cold. It's often enough to just run a heater overnight, but that all depends on where you live and how early the plants were started. Plants won't grow if it's too cold (between 5°C to 7°C (41°F to 44°F) during the day and 0°C (32°F) at night) but they're not likely to suffer otherwise. An occasional chillier day is not catastrophic, but it is better to wait and not move the plants until daytime temperatures in the greenhouse reach 15°C (59°F) or so. Monitor your max-min thermometer regularly (a must-have in the greenhouse for anyone who wants to grow things reliably). If you must keep plants in the house due to inclement weather, provide them with plenty of light by hanging fluorescent cold-white tubes at about 30 cm to 50 cm (12 to 20 inches) above the plants.

# Watering and feeding

Food supplied by high quality, nutrient rich planting soil is enough to hold the plants for several weeks. If you bought a lower-grade planting mix, however, you will need to start watering with a fertilizer mix sooner. The need for extra food depends also on the sort of plant you're growing. If the plant is to be put in a greenhouse or in a flower bed after three to four weeks, it probably won't require extra fertilizing. However, if it stays in a pot longer than this or if it's a vigorous plant such as nicotiana sylvestris (woodland tobacco), Brugmansia (angel's trumpet) or a large marigold, you will need to start feeding it after three or four weeks. You'll notice if nutrients are missing because the plant tops turn lighter green or yellowish. This can also happen because the environment is too dry or when there's a sudden cold snap. If you're unsure of the cause, try to water the plant with a light fertilizing solution and check to see if it looks greener after a few days.

## Water regularly

Water your plants sparingly without letting them dry out completely. If the plants start to droop, it's because the soil is too dry, since water keeps the plant upright and engorges the leaves. Refresh drooping plants with plain water until they perk up, and then add fertilized water. While drooping plants will not grow, it's still necessary to let the soil dry out without becoming tinder dry, as a continuously humid soil encourages fungus gnats to thrive.

Different plants have different watering needs, so it's necessary to test the soil by poking a finger into it. Some plants become tall and leggy when overwatered. Cucumbers, impatiens, and melons require a lot of moisture, whereas tomatoes and geraniums need less watering. You can't use drip irrigation during seed starting, but you can water from the bottom up. The most common method is that relied upon by professional growers, using a rimmed table which is covered by a felt mat. Water is set to drip automatically onto the mat, or you can pour water on it manually. The plants absorb water from the mat, which can stay humid for a long time. (You can also use this system to make the felt mat act as a wick, drawing water from a container.)

Both methods make it necessary to check the plants regularly. Due to slight variations in location on the table top, plants along the edges tend dry out quicker than others; some plants will be in a draft, whereas others face a more direct sun; then there are those that are exposed to too much humidity. Tables can be like large rimmed trays, but it's also common to see plants along single rows in plastic tunnels.

## Pinching and spacing

When the time comes to place them in the greenhouse, seedlings are, at this point, small plants in large containers. The pots are kept close together and are protected from the cold. As the plants grow and the weather warms up, the plants will require more space between them. They need to be moved apart so they have room to grow evenly all around (see above picture). If they're too close together they can only grow vertically, making them tall and leggy. Properly spaced, the empty area between each pot should be the same as the size of one pot. Your planting area should look like a chessboard with full and empty squares when it is finished. It follows that the larger the plant, the bigger space required between the pots so that the plants can grow sturdy. Very large plants such as nicotiana sylvestris (woodland tobacco), giant marigold, as well as tomatoes and cucumbers, need extra large spaces between them.

To encourage your plants' strong growth, follow tips and tricks from professional growers, one of which being: water sparingly. The pros allow plants to dry out a little between each watering, which means they don't let them grow too vigorously. Also, temperature is critical: if it's too hot, the plants will bolt, which is why the ambient temperature should be kept around 15°C to 16°C (59°F to 61°F).

Another important grower trick is pinching. When you pinch—that is, when you cut off the top shoot—the plant usually produces two new shoots and grows to a sturdier size. A plant that has had its top shoot pinched off several times during its growth will become very lush. That said, not all plants benefit from pinching, as it can hamper the flowering cycle. Geranium started from seed is one of the plants that does not do well from pinching.

Many plants grow flower buds early, and these are good candidates for pinching, especially impatiens and small marigolds. Those plants grow more vigorously and sturdier if the flower buds are removed.

*Protection against the sun and nighttime frost for young plants.*

*Small plants that can be spaced close together.*

A 3 cm (1") high Impatiens in bloom is not pretty, and its growth will be stunted. If the plant is allowed to flower it will produce less shoots and leaves, as all the energy is concentrated towards the flowers.

The seed packet should indicate whether a plant benefits from pinching. Plants such as ageratum (whiteweed), petunia annual dahlia, verbena, and summer phlox need to have their top shoots pinched. The plants will be far more bountiful, even though they will flower a tad later.

## Hardening off in the greenhouse

The seeds you sow and the seedlings you pot up indoors get reduced light in which to grow. If they're placed in a greenhouse, there's more daylight and cooler nights—sometimes significantly cooler. This will shock the plants if they aren't hardened-off first. When seedlings and plants are moved from an indoor climate to a greenhouse environment, they need to adjust to their new surroundings gradually. This process has to be repeated when they're ready to be moved from the greenhouse and into the garden.

The best time to move plants to the greenhouse is when the weather is overcast yet still reasonably warm.  During their first few days in the greenhouse plants need to be kept in the shade, because natural sunlight is far stronger than the soft indoor light. A thin fabric cloth can be hung over the plant and used as a shade cover. The cloth is light and can be set up temporarily over some shelving, or more permanently on casters so that it can be moved back and forth.

A mini greenhouse glass or cloche cover offers protection against frigid night temperatures. You can place a thin cloth on top of the cover to guard against the sun and it won't weigh down the plants.

*A move from kitchen to greenhouse. Many small (some a bit leggy) plants will benefit from more growth light, but will still need protection from harsh direct sunlight.*

## Hardening off and transplanting out

When you start seeds and plantings, it's very important to harden off the plants for optimal results. When the plants are big enough to move outside it will take at least a week for them to harden and to get used to their new environment. Greenhouse plants have been more protected with humidity, warmth, and filtered sunlight, so they need to be further protected from strong sunlight when they are moved outside. Thus, an overcast, warm and calm day is an ideal time for their move, preferably to a place out of a draft, as even a gusty wind can be detrimental.

Plants will gradually get used to sun but still need a thin protective cloth during the first few days. Their leaves will become more thick-skinned and will therefore cope better with both sun and wind. For example, sun-loving plants such as geraniums develop much darker leaves when they grow in full sun, but they can't handle being moved directly

*Sturdy greenhouse plants soon ready for transplanting out. They will need a week of hardening-off to get used to their new environment.*

outside into direct sunlight. They burn in the sun—much like people getting sunburned at the beach. The leaves, which naturally turn towards the sun, are easily fried, which damages their function and compromises the overall health of the plant.

Plants also need to get used to lower temperatures, which can be done by placing them outside during daylight hours and moving them back inside at night. They can be left outside during warm nights. During the first few nights the plants should be placed near a wall for protection, perhaps covered by a thin cloth cover. Hardening-off doesn't work in linear fashion: if there is an unexpected or sudden cold snap, hard frost or freeze, the plants should be moved inside—even those that have already spent a few nights outside. Let your thermometer and the weather forecast be your guides, as they can warn you of falling temperatures, and tell you specifically how cold it is or is going to be. Clear, warm days are often followed by chilly nights, especially when there is a full moon. On the other hand, overcast days followed by overcast nights are often warm, since the cloud cover acts as a barrier preventing the warmth from the earth from dispersing into the atmosphere.

This system can work even for the impatient among us who move all the plants outside without letting them go through a hardening-off period. However, the risk is greater that the plants stop growing and don't start again until after several weeks. They will come back when they are used to the new environment, but their first leaves will probably turn yellow. Some plants are more sensitive than others, like cucumber, impatiens, beans, morning glory and other plants with large, thin leaves. Marigolds and cabbage, however, are hardier and can cope quite well with sudden environmental changes.

# 5

# SUMMER FLOWERS FOR OUTDOOR PLANTINGS

There are myriad delightful summer blooms; they come in all colors and shapes to fill in flower beds, container plantings and bouquets. What's more, they're an affordable luxury—seeds are not expensive so they allow us to indulge in lavish plantings.

Summer blooms—or flowers—is used as an all-purpose term to cover lots of different plants—usually annuals, but it can also include perennials, bulbs, corms, tubers and rhizomes (collectively known as geophytes), and semi-shrubs, all of which embellish the garden in the summer. Climate dictates where and how the flowers will grow and where they should be planted. Most summer blooms do not survive cold spells and snaps; this means that the flowering stops at the first sign of frost. The advantage of starting plants from seed indoors is that you can enjoy earlier flowers and a longer flowering period.

Some summer blooms, like Heliotrope, can be challenging, as they require long pre-planting preparation; others, like calendula are easily started. Plants, when started indoors and then planted in the garden, are usually referred to as transplants. Summer blooms can be transplants as well as direct-sown flowers, such as the cornflower. There is a heightened interest in growing summer blooms among hobby gardeners, resulting in more and more seeds and varieties becoming available for sale. Furthermore, shopping for seeds is easy and fast over the Internet, since they travel well and weigh very little. Don't get taken in by the hype surrounding expensive newcomers, however—seed catalogues do tend to exaggerate their virtues.

## Separate groups

Summer blooms can be divided into separate groups: flowers that propagate through vegetative reproduction using cuttings, corms, rhizomes, and bulbs, or through division; those that can propagate through both seeds and cuttings; and finally, those that can only be propagated through seeds.

Apart from differences in propagation, there are separate kinds of seedling growth. Many traditional transplanted plants require longer pre-cultivation periods. Petunia, annual phlox, dianthus, and different varieties of salvia like to take their time, while Marigolds grow much quicker. Thanks to a seedling start in the greenhouse, you can coax early blooms from more common varieties to make a nice addition to flower beds, which can then be planned to make a beautiful early flowering ensemble. You can also try unusual plants and create unique combinations. Indoor seed starting produces many plants from just one seed packet, so you'll have the opportunity to decorate the garden lavishly, to make lush container plantings and flower beds where it would otherwise be challenging to get something to grow. It's a really affordable pleasure too because you get so many flowers on even a small budget.

*All flowers were grown in the greenhouse. Amaranth is in the middle, surrounded by light red scarlet monkey flower, yellow and red snapdragon, pink dianthus and yellow marigold in one wonderful mix.*

*A store-bought marguerite shares space with nicotiana 'tinkerbell' started from seed, and petunia.*

## Early spring

There usually isn't a lot of heat or light in a hobby greenhouse, which means that some plants simply can't be grown in that environment. You can select some plants to start growing from seed, while acquiring others from garden centers and nurseries. There is a large color palette to choose from if you decide to grow snapdragon, scarlet monkey flower, and trumpet flower. Once you've gained some experience, you can try raising more demanding plants. Growing a large and robust crop of petunias, for example, is not exactly child's play and will meet your challenge.

The most difficult part of seed starting is to know when to begin. Timing depends on when the plants are to be transplanted, so it's necessary to count backwards. In the south of Sweden, you can transplant out as early as the end of April, while in the north you have to wait until midsummer.

The light exerts a strong influence, too. If the seeds are sown in February, it could take as long as fifteen weeks for Petunia seedlings to grow large enough for transplanting; if sown in April they may only take eight weeks. The later in the season the sowing is done, the lighter and warmer the environment will be, thus the faster the seeds will grow.

How large the plants typically grow before transplanting affects your sowing date. It is best if plants have grown a bit but have not yet reached the flowering stage before they are planted out. Totally green plants take root quicker and adjust faster to their new environment. A flower in bloom, on the other hand, might stop growing because of the shock of being moved outside from the greenhouse. This means that it can stop flowering, during which time the green plant can catch up and flower earlier. When buying plants, you'll want to see flowers so you know what color and type of flower to expect. If you start seeds yourself, however, you'll already know what you've got so the plants don't have to be in bloom.

## How is it done?

Seed starting and potting up follow the same steps, whether it be flowers or vegetables. The differences lie mostly in growth times and the size of pots to use when potting up. Some plants also need pinching to grow sturdy, while pinching is hardly ever necessary with vegetables. All plants follow, on the whole, the order described here. Further details about soil, water, and fertilizing can be found in the section about seed starting and planting, on page 29. There you'll also find a detailed description on how to sow seeds and how to pot up into bigger containers.

The best way to start the seeds is inside your house. With few exceptions, most seeds need warmth to grow. A room temperature of 20°C to 25°C (68°F to 77°F) works well; put the seed tray in a window that gets good light exposure, and it won't need to be moved into the greenhouse until there is green showing. In some cases this means the seed tray will stay in the house for two to four weeks before it needs to be moved out. The date at which you can start the seeds depends on when you can transfer them to the greenhouse, which in turn depends on the weather. If you have a fan heater, you might be able to move the seedlings into the greenhouse earlier.

Some seeds, like impatiens, summer geranium, and snapdragon, require light to germinate, so their seeds cannot be covered with soil. To prevent the soil surface from drying out, you'll need to cover the seeds with plastic or glass, or use a mini greenhouse.

Then there are seeds that need stratification through chilling before they can germinate—nature has placed barriers in the seed to prevent it from germinating at the wrong time of the year. Some seeds require total darkness; yet others must bask in at least twelve hours of light per day. Reputable seed sellers have information about special requirements printed on the seed packets. Most plants, however, aren't complicated and can be sown following the instructions above.

## What to choose and what to steer clear of

One of winter's great pleasures is to browse through seed catalogs. If you order seeds well in advance they should arrive by January or February.

Once you've decided which plants you'd like to start from seed, you'll need to figure out the right time to start each type of seed. A good way to do this is to stagger the sowing of different seeds in order to avoid having to care for everything all at once. (The seeds themselves don't take up much space, but the seedlings will eventually need to be potted up and then space might become an issue.) With this in mind, sort the seed packets into three groups:

◆ Plants that need a long period of time indoors with lots of light in order to bloom—twelve to sixteen weeks not being unusual.
◆ Plants that need less time—about six to ten weeks—and where success is more likely.
◆ Plants that can be directly sown, but which will offer up better results and earlier blooms if started inside.

Some plants need to be propagated through cuttings in order to be able to grow true. True versions of fuchsia and geraniums, as well as many wave petunias, blue potato bush, daisies and angels trumpet can be bought as small or big plants.

## Table of summer flowers

The following pages can help you plan your garden, and can be used as a guide to plants that can be started from seed indoors. In these lists you'll find the name and the botanical name in alphabetical order, in addition to the amount of time it takes each plant to germinate.

Suitable germination temperatures will be noted on the seed packet—it's usually around 20°C to 25°C (68°F to 77°F). You can start the seeds anytime in the spring, depending when you'd like to see them bloom. Most plant seeds are sown in March and April, with a few earlier in January and February.

Growing time, as stated in the list, is from the time the seed is sown until the plant is ready for out-planting. This doesn't necessarily mean the plant is in flower—that can take several months depending on the plant variety. The guideline is not to be followed too strictly: it's sometimes acceptable to plant out both earlier or later than the listed time—it will depend on weather conditions.

The preferred growing temperature is noted, too, but again it's occasionally open to variation. Most plants thrive in 15°C to 18°C (59°F to 64°F). The cooler and darker the plants' environment, the longer it will take them to grow. It doesn't matter if the plants are on the small side at first—they'll quickly catch up once they're transplanted outside.

*Mini greenhouses—that is, plastic boxes with transparent covers—are excellent for sowing and pre-cultivation indoors. Early seed starting in the kitchen.*

# Indoor seed starting and pre-cultivation for summer flowers

Plants with an asterisk (*) beside their name can be direct-sown in a flower bed and will still have time to flower—in the south of Sweden at least.

| PLANT NAME<br>Swedish, **English**, *Scientific* | Sow<br>Month | Weeks to<br>germination | Cultivation<br>in weeks | Cultivation<br>temperature |
|---|---|---|---|---|
| Klockmalva—**Flowering maple**, *Abutilon x hybridum* | February | 1 | 14–16 | 18°C–21°C (64.4°F–69.8°F) |
| Parakrasse—**Paracress (toothache plant)**, *Acmelia oleracea* | March | 1 | 12–14 | 18°C–24°C (64.4°F–75.2°F) |
| Anisisop—**Anise hyssop**, *Agastache* | March–April | 3 | 10–12 | 15°C–18°C (59°F–64.4°F) |
| Ageratum—**Mexian paintbrush**, *Ageratum houstonianum* | March–April | 1–2 | 10–12 | 15°C–18°C (59°F–64.4°F) |
| Papegojblad—**Red threads**, *Alternanthera ficoidea* | March–April | 0–1 | 10–12 | 18°C–20°C (64.4°F–68°F) |
| Amarant, Rävsvans—**Foxtail amaranth (Love lies bleeding)**, *Amaranthus** | March–April | 2 | 9–10 | 20°C–24°C (68°–75.2°F) |
| Afrikansk Oxtunga—**Cape forget-me-not**, *Anchusa capensis** | March–April | 1–2 | 9–10 | 15°C–18°C (59°F–64.4°F) |
| Angelonia—**Summer snapdragon**, *Angelonia angustifolia* | Feb–April | 1 | 14–16 | 20°C–24°C (68°F–75.2°F) |
| Lejongap—**Common snapdragon**, *Antirrhinum majus** | March–April | 1–2 | 10 | 12°C–15°C (53.6°F–59°F) |
| Sommarcypress—**Ragweed**, *Bassia scoparia* | March | 1–2 | 9–12 | 15°C–18°C (59°F–64.4°F) |
| Begonia, sommar—**Wax begonia**, *Begonia x semperfl.* | Feb–March | 2–3 | 12–14 | 18°C–20°C (64.4°F–68°F) |
| Begonia drakving—**Begonia dragonwing**, *Begonia hybrid Dragon Wing* | Feb | 2–3 | 14–22 | 18°C–20°C (64.4°F–68°F) |
| Begonia, knöl—**Tuberous begonia**, *Begonia x tuberhybrida* | January | 2–3 | 20–22 | 18°C–20°C (64.4°F–68°F) |
| Ampelskära—**Fernleaved beggarticks**, *Bidens ferulifol* | March | 1–2 | 12–14 | 15°C–18°C (59°F–64.4°F) |
| Dockkrage—**Swan river daisy**, *Brachyscome iberidifolia* | March–April | 1–2 | 9–10 | 15°C–18°C (59°F–64.4°F) |
| Prydnadskål—**Ornamental cabbage**, *Brassica oleracea**–later seed starting for fall plants | April | 0–1 | 10–12 | 12°C–15°C (53.6°F–59°F) |
| Sommaraster—**China aster**, *Callistephus chinensis** | March–April | 1–2 | 12–16 | 15°C–18°C (59°F–64.4°F) |
| Plymört—**Plumed cockscomb**, *Celosia argentea* | March | 1–2 | 10–12 | 18°C–20°C (64.4°F–68°F) |
| Vaxblomma—**Wax flower, honeywort**, *Cerinthe* | March–April | 1–2 | 10–12 | 15°C–18°C (59°F–64.4°F) |
| Paradisblomster—**Spiderplant**, *Cleome hassleriana** | March | 1–2 | 10–12 | 15°C–18°C (59°F–64.4°F) |
| Klockranka—**Cup-and-saucer-vine**, *Cobaea scandens* | March–April | 2–3 | 10 | 15°C–18°C (59°F–64.4°F) |
| Riddarsporre, romersk—**Delphinium, rocket larkspur**, *Consolida ajacis** | March | 2–3 | 9–10 | 15°C–18°C (59°F–64.4°F) |
| Riddarsporre—**Field larkspur**, *Consolida regalis** | March | 2–3 | 9–10 | 15°C–18°C (59°F–64.4°F) |
| Flicköga—**Coreopsis, large-flowered tickseed**, *Coreopsis grandiflora* | Feb–March | 1–2 | 12–16 | 15°C–18°C (59°F–64.4°F) |
| Tigeröga—**Plains coreopsis**, *Coreopsis tintoria** | March–April | 2 | 10–12 | 15°C–18°C (59°F–64.4°F) |
| Rosenskära—**Garden cosmos, Mexican aster**, *Cosmos bipinnatus* | April–May | 1–2 | 10–12 | 15°C–18°C (59°F–64.4°F) |
| Gullskära—**Yellow cosmos**, *Cosmos sulphureus* | April–May | 1–2 | 8–10 | 15°C–18°C (59°F–64.4°F) |
| Cigarettglöd—**Cigar plant, Mexican cigar**, *Cuphea ignea* | March | 1–2 | 10–12 | 15°C–18°C (59°F–64.4°F) |
| Sommardahlia—**Dahlia pinnata**, *Dahlia x pinnata* | Feb–April | 1–2 | 12–14 | 15°C–18°C (59°F–64.4°F) |
| Spikklubba, indisk—**Devil's trumpet, metel**, *Datura metel* | Jan–April | 1–2 | 10–20 | 15°C–18°C (59°F–64.4°F) |
| Nejlika, borst—**Sweet William**, *Dianthus barbatus-gr** | March | 1–2 | 12–14 | 15°C–18°C (59°F–64.4°F) |
| Nejlika, trädgårds—**Carnation**, *Dianthus caryophyllus* | Feb–March | 1 | 12–16 | 15°C–18°C (59°F–64.4°F) |
| Nejlika, sommar—**China pink, India pink**, *Diantus chinensis* | March | 1–2 | 12–14 | 13°C–15°C (55.4°F–59°F) |
| Tvillingsporre—**Twinspur**, *Diascia* | Feb–March | 1 | 10–16 | 15°C–18°C (59°F–64.4°F) |
| Silvernjurvinda—**Silver pony's foot, silver nickel vine**, *Dichandra argentea* | Feb–April | 1 | 12–14 | 20°C–24°C (68°F–75.2°F) |
| Fingerborgsblomma—**Foxglove, annual**, *Digitalis* | Feb–March | 1–2 | 12–14 | 15°C–18°C (59°F–64.4°F) |
| Doroteablomma—**Livingstone daisy**, *Dorotheanthus* | March | 1–2 | 10–14 | 15°C–18°C (59°F–64.4°F) |
| Fackelranka—**Chilean glory vine**, *Eccremocarpus scaber* | March–April | 2 | 8–10 | 15°C–18°C (59°F–64.4°F) |
| Murbinka—**Mexican fleabane, Spanish daisy**, *Erigeran karvinskianus* | March | 1 | 12–14 | 15°C–18°C (59°F–64.4°F) |
| Gyllenlack, ettårig—**Wallflower, annual**, *Erysimum* | March | 1 | 11–12 | 13°C–18°C (55.4°–64.4°F) |
| Eukalyptus—**Eucalyptus**, *Eucalyptus* | Jan–Feb | 2–3 | 20–22 | 15°C–18°C (59°F–64.4°F) |

*Common snapdragon is a low-growing variety that is easy to start from seed and flowers quite early.*

| PLANT NAME<br>Swedish, **English**, *Scientific* | Sow<br>Month | Weeks to<br>germination | Cultivation<br>in weeks | Cultivation<br>temperature |
|---|---|---|---|---|
| Zuluaster—**Kingfisher daisy, true blue daisy**, *Felicia heterophylla* | March | 2–3 | 10–12 | 15°C–18°C (59°F–64.4°F) |
| Bronsfänkäl—**Common fennel**, *Foeniculum vulgare\** | March–April | 2 | 10–12 | 10°C–15°C (50°F–59°F) |
| Fuchsia, flerårig—**Hybrid fuchsia, perennial**, *Fuchsia x hybrida* | February | 2 | 20–22 | 18°C–20°C (64.4°F–68°F) |
| Kockardblomster—**Blanket flower**, *Gaillardia* | March | 2–3 | 12–15 | 15°C–18°C (59°F–64.4°F) |
| Påfågelsblomster—**African daisy, treasure flower**, *Gazania* | Feb–March | 2–3 | 12–16 | 15°C–18°C (59°F–64.4°F) |
| Grusnejlika, murslöja—**Baby's breath**, *Gypsophila muralis* | March | 0–1 | 10–12 | 15°C–18°C (59°F–64.4°F) |
| Sommarsolbrud—**Yellow sneezeweed, bitter sneezeweed**, *Helenium amarum* | March | 0–1 | 10–12 | 20°C–24°C (68°F–75.2°F) |
| Solros—**Sunflower**, *Helianthus annuus\** | April | 2 | 6–10 | 15°C–18°C (59°F–64.4°F) |
| Rabatteternell—**Licorice plant, trailing dusty miller**, *Helichrysum petiolare* | Feb–March | 3 | 12–14 | 18°C–24°C (64.4°F–75.2°F) |
| Heliotrop—**Garden heliotrope**, *Heliotropium arborescens* | March | 2–4 | 12–15 | 15°C–18°C (59°F–64.4°F) |
| Hibiskus, blod—**Cranberry hibiscus**, *Hibiscus acetosella* | Feb–March | 1–2 | 12–14 | 18°C–20°C (64.4°F–68°F) |
| Hibiskus, prakt—**Rose mallow, swamp mallow**, *Hibiscus moscheutos-gr.* | Jan–Feb | 1–2 | 14–16 | 21°C–24°C (69.8°F–75.2°F) |
| Japansk humle—**Japanese hop**, *Humulus japonicus* | April | 2 | 6–10 | 15°C–18°C (59°F–64.4°F) |
| Roseniberis—**Candytuft**, *Iberis umbellata\** | April | 1 | 8–10 | 15°C–18°C (59°F–64.4°F) |
| Comorobalsamin—**African impatiens**, *Impatiens auricoma* | Feb–March | 1–2 | 14–16 | 21°C–24°C (69.8°F–75.2°F) |
| Lyckliga Lotta—**New Guinea Impatiens**, *Impatiens hawkeri* | Feb–March | 1–3 | 12–14 | 20°C–24°C (68°F–75.2°F) |
| Flitiga Lisa—**Busy Lizzie impatiens**, *Impatiens walleriana* | March–April | 1–3 | 10–12 | 15°C–18°C (59°F–64.4°F) |
| Spanska flaggan—**Firecracker vine, Spanish flag**, *Ipomoea lobata* | Feb–March | 1–3 | 12–14 | 18°C–20°C (64.4°F–68°F) |
| Fjäderstjärnvinda—**Cypress vine**, *Ipomoea quamoclit* | March–April | 2 | 12–14 | 18°C–20°C (64.4°F–68°F) |
| Blomman för dagen—**Morning glory**, *Ipomoea tricolor* | March–April | 2 | 12–14 | 18°C–20°C (64.4°F–68°F) |
| Höblomster—**Blood leaf, gizzard plant**, *Iresine herbstii* | March | 1 | 10–12 | 18°C–24°C (64.4°F–75.2°F) |
| Hjälmböna—**Hyacinth bean**, *Lablab purpureus* | March | 1–2 | 10–12 | 18°C–20°C (64.4°F–68°F) |
| Luktärt—**Sweet pea**, *Lathyrus odoratus\** | April–May | 2–3 | 5–10 | 15°C–18°C (59°F–64.4°F) |
| Blå stjärnlobelia—**Blue Laurentia**, *Laurentia axillaris* | Jan–Feb | 2–3 | 16 -20 | 15°C–18°C (59°F–64.4°F) |
| Färgsporre—**Toadflax, (maroccana)**, *Linaria\** | March–April | 1 | 9–10 | 15°C–18°C (59°F–64.4°F) |
| Lobelia, kant–häng—**Lobelia, edging, hanging baskets**, *Lobelia erinus* | March | 2–3 | 7–10 | 15°C–18°C (59°F–64.4°F) |
| Lobelia, rabatt—**Lobelia, bedding plant**, *Lobelia x speciosa* | Jan–Feb | 2–3 | 16–20 | 15°C–18°C (59°F–64.4°F) |
| Strandkrassing—**Sweet alyssum**, *Lobularia maritima\** | March | 1–2 | 8–10 | 12°C–15°C (53.6°F–59°F) |
| Sommarlövkoja—**Brompton stock, hoary stock**, *Matthiola incana* | March | 1–2 | 10–14 | 10°C–13°C (50°F–55.4°F) |
| Lejongapsranka—**Creeping gloxinia, climbing foxglove**, *Lophospermum* | March–April | 1–2 | 6–10 | 15°C–18°C (59°F–64.4°F) |
| Maurandia—**Climbing snapdragon**, *Maurandia (Asarina)* | March–April | 1–2 | 6–10 | 15°C–18°C (59°F–64.4°F) |
| Pysslingkrage—**Mini marguerite, annual chrysanthemum**, *Mauranthemum paludosum\** | March | 1–2 | 8–11 | 15°C (59°F |
| Gyckelblomma—**Monkey flower**, *Mimulus* | April | 1–2 | 6–10 | 8°C–12°C (46.4°F–53.6°F) |
| Irlandsklockor; musselsyska—**Bells of Ireland**, *Moluccella laevis* | March | 2–3 | 8–10 | 12°C–15°C (53.6°F–59°F) |
| Doftnemesia—**Nemesia**, *Nemesia caerulea* | March | 1 | 10–12 | 18°C–20°C (64.4°F–68°F) |
| Nemesia—**Cape jewels**, *Nemesia strumosa\** | March | 1–2 | 10–14 | 10°C–15°C (50°F–59°F) |
| Klocktobak—**Langsdorff's tobacco**, *Nicotiana langsdorffii* | March | 2–3 | 10–14 | 15°C–18°C (59°F–64.4°F) |
| Blomstertobak—**Winged tobacco, jasmine tobacco**, *Nicotiana sanderae* | March | 1–2 | 10–12 | 15°C–18°C (59°F–64.4°F) |
| Narcisstobak—**Woodland tobacco**, *Nicotiana sylvestris* | Feb–March | 1–2 | 13–15 | 15°C–18°C (59°F–64.4°F) |
| Nierembergia—**Cupflower**, *Nierembergia hippomanica* | March | 1–2 | 12–14 | 15°C–18°C (59°F–64.4°F) |
| Zonalpelargon—**Zonal geranium, bedding geranium**, *Pelargonium x hortorum* | Jan–Feb | 1–2 | 20–22 | 15°C–18°C (59°F–64.4°F) |
| Hängpelargon—**Ivy geranium, cascading geranium**, *Pelargonium peltatum* | Jan–Feb | 1–2 | 20–22 | 15°C–18°C (59°F–64.4°F) |
| Purpurhatt, Penstemon, Skäggört—**Beardtongue**, *Penstemon* | Feb–March | 2–3 | 12–18 | 12°C–15°C (53.6°F–59°F) |
| Bladmynta—**Perilla, Beefsteak plant**, *Perillo frutescens* | March | 2 | 8–12 | 15°C–18°C (59°F–64.4°F) |

*Sweet peas need a lot of time to germinate. Soak the seeds in water overnight, sow and start from seed to enjoy early flowers. This variety is called 'Blue Ripple'.*

| PLANT NAME<br>Swedish, **English**, *Scientific* | Sow<br>Month | Weeks to<br>germination | Cultivation<br>in weeks | Cultivation<br>temperature |
|---|---|---|---|---|
| Ampelpilört, slingerpilört–**Pink knotweed, Japanese knotweed,** *Persicaria capitata* | March | 2–3 | 8–12 | 10°C–12°C (50°F–53.6°F) |
| Petunia, vanlig–**Petunia, garden petunia,** *Petunia x hybrida* | March | 1–2 | 10–12 | 15°C–18°C (59°F–64.4°F) |
| Petunia, mini–**Petunia milliflora fantasy,** *Petunia x hybrida* | March–April | 1–2 | 8–10 | 14°C–16°C (57.2°F–60.8°F) |
| Praktpetunia–**Spreading petunia, wave,** *Petunia x hybrida* | Feb–March | 1–2 | 12–16 | 18°C–24°C (64.4°F–75.2°F) |
| Sommarflox–**Annual phlox, Drummond's phlox,** *Phlox drummondii* | March | 1–2 | 10–12 | 15°C–18°C (59°F–64.4°F) |
| Silverljus–**Silver spurflower,** *Piectranthus argentatus* | Feb–March | 1–2 | 14–16 | 21°C–24°C (69.8°F–75.2°F) |
| Praktportlak–**Moss rose purslane, moss rose,** *Portulaca grandiflora* | March | 1–2 | 8–12 | 15°C–18°C (59°F–64.4°F) |
| Törnrosas kjortel–**Purple bell vine,** *Rhodochiton atrosanguineum* | March–April | 1–2 | 8–12 | 15°C–18°C (59°F–64.4°F) |
| Ricin–**Castor bean,** *Ricinus communis* | March | 2–3 | 10–12 | 15°C–18°C (59°F–64.4°F) |
| Rudbeckia, sommar–**Black-eyed Susan,** *Rudbeckia hirta* | March | 1–2 | 12–16 | 15°C–18°C (59°F–64.4°F) |
| Trumpetblomma–**Velvet trumpet flower, painted tongue,** *Salpiglossis sinuata* | March | 1 | 10–12 | 12°C–15°C (53.6°F–59°F) |
| Salvia, scharlakans–**Scarlet sage, Texas sage,** *Salvia coccinea* | March–April | 1–2 | 11–13 | 15°C–18°C (59°F–64.4°F) |
| Salvia, dagg–**Mealy blue sage,** *Salvia farinacea* | March | 1–2 | 11–13 | 15°C–18°C (59°F–64.4°F) |
| Salvia, blå–**Gentian sage,** *Salvia patens* | Jan–March | 1–2 | 10–13 | 15°C–18°C (59°F–64.4°F) |
| Salvia, prakt–**Tropical sage,** *Salvia splendens* | March | 1–2 | 10–12 | 15°C–18°C (59°F–64.4°F) |
| Salvia, brok–**Clary, red-topped sage,** *Salvia viridis** | March–April | 2–3 | 8–12 | 15°C–18°C (59°F–64.4°F) |
| Grå helgonört–**Cotton lavender,** *Santolina chamaecyparissus* | February | 5–8 | 15–20 | 5°C–10° C (41°F–50°F) |
| Husarknappar–**Creeping zinnia,** *Sanvitalia procumbens* | March | 2 | 10–14 | 15°C–18°C (59°F–64.4°F) |
| Fjärilsblomster–**Butterfly flower,** *Schizanthus pinnatus** | March–April | 2–3 | 8–9 | 15°C–18°C (59°F–64.4°F) |
| Silverek–**Dusty miller, Silver dust,** *Senecio cineraria* | March (sow later for fall planting) | 1–2 | 10–12 | 15°C–18°C (59°F–64.4°F) |
| Palettblad–**Coleus,** *Solenostemon scutellarioides* | March | 1–2 | 10–14 | 18°C–20°C (64.4°F–68°F) |
| Tagetes, stor–**Mexican marigold, Aztec marigold,** *Tagetes erecta* | March | 1–2 | 10–11 | 15°C–18°C (59°F–64.4°F) |
| Tagetes, sammets–**French marigold,** *Tagetes patula* | March–April | 1 | 8–10 | 15°C–18°C (59°F–64.4°F) |
| Tagetes, liten–**Signet marigold,** *Tagetes tenuifolia** | March–April | 1 | 8–10 | 15°C–18°C (59°F–64.4°F) |
| Mattram–**Feverfew,** *Tanacetum parthenium* | Feb–March | 2–3 | 12–14 | 15°C–18°C (59°F–64.4°F) |
| Silverkrage–**Silver lace bush,** *Tanacetum ptarmiciflorum* | March | 1–2 | 13–15 | 15°C–18°C (59°F–64.4°F) |
| Svartöga–**Black-eyed Susan vine,** *Thunbergia alata* | March–April | 1–2 | 10–12 | 15°C–18°C (59°F–64.4°F) |
| Inkakrage–**Mexican sunflower,** *Tithonia rotundifolia** | Feb–March | 2–3 | 12–14 | 15°C–18°C (59°F–64.4°F) |
| Sommarhalsört–**Blue throatwort,** *Trachelium caeruleum* | March | 2 | 12–18 | 15°C–18°C (59°F–64.4°F) |
| Fjärilskrasse–**Canary creeper,** *Tropaeolum peregrinum** | April | 1–2 | 6–10 | 15°C–18°C (59°F–64.4°F) |
| Trädgårdskungsljus,–**Mullein, flannel Plant, 'Southern Charum,'** *Verbascum* | Feb–March | 1 | 14–16 | 15°C–18°C (59°F–64.4°F) |
| Verbena, jätte–**Tall verbena,** *Verbena banariensis* | Jan–Feb | 2–5 | 15–20 | 15°C–18°C (59°F–64.4°F) |
| Verbena, doft–**Rose verbena,** *Glaudularia (verbena) canadensis* | March | 2–3 | 12–14 | 15°C–18°C (59°F–64.4°F) |
| Verbena, viol–**Slender vervain,** *Verbena rigida* | Feb–March | 2–4 | 12–14 | 15°C–18°C (59°F–64.4°F) |
| Verbena, trädgårds–**Garden vervain,** *Glaudularia (verbena) x hybrida* | Feb–March | 2–3 | 13–15 | 15°C–18°C (59°F–64.4°F) |
| Zinnia–**Zinnia, youth-and-old-age,** *Zinnia elegans** | March–April | 1–2 | 10–12 | 15°C–28°C (59°F–82.4°F) ? |

Black-eyed susan flowers late in summer if direct-seeded. Pre-cultivation in-house will make them bloom earlier. Every fall seeds are collected from this old-timer, and are set aside for spring sowing.

*Abundant flowering beauty on a sunny step. The mini-petunia 'million bells' is propagated through cuttings.*

## Summer flowers for different sites

You can try many different and tempting new plants by starting seeds indoors, but you must still take into consideration the outdoor site where the plant is going to end up growing. Summer flowers don't all thrive in similar locations—most of the richly flowering plants need abundant sunshine, plenty of soil, water, and nutrients, while others will tolerate tougher conditions.

It can get hot, dry and perhaps windy for window and balcony boxes on south-facing decks or steps. There you'll have to put plants that can stand up to searing heat over several hours; geraniums and twinspur are examples of hardy blooms that can weather these kinds of conditions. Cut-leaved daisy, yellow cosmos, creeping zinnia, and licorice plant are also surprisingly tough and large, and won't be as colorful and lush with flowers if placed in the shade. Fuchsia, ornamental bacopa, impatiens, and geraniums, on the other hand, make excellent shade plants. Nicotiana, New Guinea impatiens and most leafy plants also do well in the shade.

## Shuffle and Deal

Seed starting, aside from allowing you to try a lot of plants that are not sold as seedlings, offers you the opportunity to put together your own flower compositions. You can use different companion plants earlier in the season in big containers to decorate your garden, before it's time to plant the flowers in the ground. Don't crowd too many plants in each pot, however, as they'll need space to grow and fully develop over the summer. Also, leave larger containers in the greenhouse warmth a little longer—the plants will grow together into an attractive entity and they'll be more uniform in size. If springtime warms up quickly, the plant's growth will explode and will go from green seedling to a flowering plant in as little as a week's time. Place the pots outside to fully enjoy those beautiful blooms.

Take pictures of the plantings, and write down the names of the plants to have on hand as reference for future plantings. Take note of the good plants as well as the lesser performing ones. The fun lies in being able to mix flower color, leaf color as well as cultivation method. Many leafy plants are used as fillers to add calm to companion-plant flowers.

## Hanging planters

The advantage of starting your own plants is that you will enjoy an abundance of flowers. A clustering of many small plants has a more beautiful visual impact than only a few big ones in a container; this is especially true for hanging planters.

Small plants are used to make English-style hanging basket planters. The planter, made of coarse netting, is lined with plastic and then moss. Plant roots are introduced from the outside through the netting holes. The planter is filled with soil bit by bit, while the sides are planted in rows. At the very top, once the planter's upper rim is reached, a sturdier and upright plant is planted, such as a tuberous begonia or summer dahlia. By all means mix several different types of plants to highlight their beauty—lobelia, creeping charlie (ground-ivy), licorice plant, impatiens, ornamental bacopa, yellow cosmos, cut-leaved daisy, mini-petunia and ivy, for example. Hanging planters require nutrient-rich, quality soil and regular watering with fertilizer each day over the summer. Many plants in relatively small baskets need a lot of nutrients and water to be able to continue flowering and growing.

To develop their full effect, hanging baskets can be planted three to four weeks before being placed outside. Use plants that have been cultivated in the greenhouse, and transplant them into

*An early, store-bought twinspur stays in the greenhouse until all risk of nighttime frost has passed.*

### Flowering plants for hanging baskets
Mexican paintbrush, *Ageratum houstonianum*
Wax begonia, *Begonia x semperflorens-cultorum*
Tuberous begonia, *Begonia x tuberhybrida*
Fern-leaved beggarticks, *Bidens ferulifolia*
Cut-leaved daisy, *Brachyscome*
Million bells, *Calibrachoa*
Calitunia, *x Calitunia*
Star of Bethlehem, *Campanula isophylla*
Blue rock bindweed, *Convolvulus sabatius*
Carnation, *Dianthus chariophyllis*
China pink, *Dianthus chinensis*
Cottage pink, *Dianthus xsemperflorens*
Twinspur, *Diascia*
Blue daisy, *Felicia heterophylla*
Hybrid fuchsia, *Fuchsia x hybrida*
African daisy, treasure flower, *Gazania*
Garden vervain, *Glandularia (Verbena) x hybrida*
New Guinea impatiens, *Impatiens hawkeri*
Busy Lizzy impatiens, *Impatiens walleriana*
Lobelia, edging, hanging baskets, *Lobelia erinus*
Sweet alyssum, *Lobularia maritima*
Nemesia, Cape Jewels, *Nemesia strumosa*
Ivy-Leaf geranium, cascading geranium, *Pelargonium peltatum*
Spreading petunia, wave, *Petunia x hybrida*
Moss rose purslane, moss rose, *Portulaca grandiflora*
Creeping zinnia, *Sanvitalia procumbens*
Black-eyed Susan vine, *Thunbergia alata*
Garden nasturtium, *Tropaeolum majus*
Canary creeper, *Tropaeolum peregrinum*
Miniature pansy, tricolor, *Viola*

### Leafy plants for hanging baskets
Bugleweed, Blue bugle, *Ajuga reptans*
English ivy, European ivy, *Hedera helix*
Curry plant, *Helichrysum italicum*
Licorice plant, *Helichysum petiolare*
Creeping lamium, Deadnettle, *Lamium*
Parrot's beak, *Lotus berthelotii*
Creeping Jenny, Moneywort, *Lysimacchia nummularia*
Parsley, *Petroselinum crispum*
Spurflower, a variety, *Plectranthus*
Cherry tomatoes, *Solanum lycopersicum*
Coleus, *Solenostemon scutellarioides*

*The larger the hanging basket, the prettier the blooms.*

hanging baskets in the spring. Leave the hanging basket in the greenhouse to let the plants branch out fully into one big plant. Use large hanging baskets, preferably holding 5 to 10 liters (1 1/4 to 2 1/2 gallons) of soil. The larger the hanging basket, the less likely it is to dry out.

## Long-blooming hanging baskets
Large, beautiful summer blooms such as cascading geraniums and wave petunias have become very popular. These sturdy plants are usually propagated through cuttings, which means you will have to buy the plants. (Some species can be cultivated from seed but it is better to buy the plants, as it takes a very long time to cultivate them.) They're sold in hanging baskets, but if they're transplanted into larger baskets they will grow even more impressive. There are special hanging baskets outfitted with large water containers that are made specifically for these huge plants. It's necessary to have large spreading wave petunias and cascading geraniums to hide the water containers, but then again these plants do require a very large amount of water and fertilizer.

Towards the end of the summer, when the plant is at its fullest, you can keep it flowering and prevent it from wilting—even if you leave home for the weekend. Typically, big plants in pots dry out quickly at the end of summer, and a weekend of neglect is enough for them to collapse. The plant is not as young and spry in the fall and cannot survive drying out. Many summer flowers that wilt and die down in August have already started to dry up or are suffering from a lack of nutrients. If you make sure they're placed in large pots and are given fertilized water regularly, they will keep flowering without any problems until first frost. Some plants, like ornamental bacopa, twinspur, and licorice plant can even survive one or two nighttime cold snaps.

## Purchasing plants

Owning a greenhouse allows one to be picky. You can buy plants for planting out early in the spring, and cultivate them in the greenhouse until it's time to transplant them outside. Spring is when you'll find the largest selection of plants at garden centers and nurseries; it's also the ideal time to discover thrilling newcomers. It's better to hold off on transplanting until the weather warms up and the risk of an overnight frost is over, because if you plant out too early, the plants will stop growing and their leaves will turn yellow. It's preferable to keep them in the greenhouse, ventilated on sunny days and sheltered from frost at night, as this will acclimatize the plants somewhat to their future life outside. If they're planted in pots and hanging baskets they will have plenty of time to grow, and thus will be hardy and healthy at transplanting time. That way you also won't have the worry about flowers and long branches getting damaged on the trip home from the garden center or nursery.

## Exotic colors

Lots of vibrantly colored plants with exotic allure originate in warmer countries. Most of them aren't perennials in Sweden, yet they've been an integral part of our gardening scene for many years. The dahlia is an example of such a plant. It requires a substantial amount of work—you can save its tubers from year to year, but they need to be planted in good soil, dug up in the fall, and then kept in a frost-free but cool environment. Despite

*Peruvian lily, also called parrot flower and its roots; a rewarding geophyte plant overwintered like a dahlia. Next page spread: Seed-started annual summer dahlia 'fireworks.'*

*It is practical to sow and plant in the greenhouse as it doesn't matter if some soil ends up on the floor.*

## Many geophytes

There are many rewarding plant bulbs that will flower beautifully if they are started early. Peruvian lily, fresia, canna, and begonia all need to start inside if they are to reach full bloom. Peacock lily and gladiolii can be planted out directly, but are also good to pre-cultivate inside to achieve earlier flowers, just like anemone and persian buttercup. Uncertain hardiness in red hot poker/torch lilies and montbretia (which are perennials in the south of Sweden) make them good candidates to be started early and overwintered inside.

Gentian sage, which gets fat white roots, as well as four o'clocks with their carrot-like roots, are, surprisingly, geophytes. They are used as annuals but are in fact perennials. They can have a long blooming period if their roots are dug up, kept free of frost, and then planted in a pot in the greenhouse early in spring.

Sage grows increasingly large year after year, and you can divide it. Four o'clocks grow into sturdy plants similar to low-growing bushes, with an abundance of small colorful flowers.

## How to's—Planting and care of geophytes

In spring, geophytes, i.e., bulbs and roots, are planted in large pots to give them plenty of space to grow. Plant them directly in attractive planters, or in large plastic pots with drainage holes. Plastic buckets with drainage holes drilled at the bottom also work perfectly well.

◆ Place a layer of nutrient-rich planting soil in the bottom of the pot or container. The depth of the layer depends on the plant; dahlias require approximately 20 cm (7 3/4").
◆ Spread out the roots or position the geophytes on the surface. Press down so there's proper contact with the soil.
◆ Cover with planting soil according to the instructions on the soil bag. Dahlia roots have to be covered, and the tips (root cap) should be about 5 cm (2") below the surface.
◆ Bulbs such as gladiolus can have more soil added little by little as they grow. Canna lilies require plenty of growing space and nutrient-rich soil.
◆ Water generously at planting time, and then more sparingly afterwards until the plants start to show green shoots.
◆ Leave the plants in a sunny spot in the greenhouse to give them time to fill in. Once the weather allows, they can be placed outside.
◆ Bury the entire pot in the flower bed, or place the decorative planter in its chosen spot.

this doting care, there's no guarantee that they'll bloom before first frost.

You'll save a lot of time if you plant the roots in large pots and let them start in the greenhouse. Dahlias usually need warm soil, which means that you cannot plant them in the central part of Sweden until the month of June; if the frost arrives by the end of August that doesn't leave you much time to enjoy the flowers. If they are started in the greenhouse, however, they can be transplanted as soon as the risk of night frost is over.

◆ Another way is to ease the plant out of the pot carefully, and plant it directly in the ground. Place the pot on its side and pull it off gently to avoid damaging the fragile plant stems.

◆ Plant the clumps—complete with stems and leaves—at approximately the same depth as in the pot. Root tips should be slightly more than an inch below the soil surface.

◆ Water and fertilize generously during the summer. Most bulb plants need a large amount of added nutrition to grow roots and bulbs in the following years.

◆ Bulbs and other geophytes are dug up in the fall, to be stored over winter according to their specific needs. If the plant has been potted, then the whole pot and plant are overwintered together, and the plant is re-potted into new, nutrient-rich soil the following spring. Another advantage of container growing is that the whole plant can be moved inside the greenhouse if there is risk of frost. As the buds open into flowers, these can then be used as cut flowers.

## Hardy lilies

Lilies are different in that many are hardy and can overwinter in the ground as long as the soil is well drained; however the large, fleshy bulbs are prone to rotting. If bought in early spring and planted in pots in the greenhouse, they will have time to get started and will produce earlier blooms. Lilies need to be planted deep in the soil, but there is a way to accelerate their growth:

◆ Plant the lily bulb in a bucket or a deep pot with a 10 cm (4") layer of soil at the bottom. Fill with soil until the bulb is covered.

◆ When the plant shows green shoots, add more soil several times as the plant grows, until the pot or bucket is filled to the brim.

◆ Once the stalk has grown above the soil surface, it can be planted carefully in the ground in its designated place.

Another method is to keep lilies potted through the whole season; in this case the pots and bulbs will need to be protected from harsh winter weather. Potted lilies are considered more or less a common 'house plant,' and are sold for decoration both inside the home and outside. Many lilies can be transplanted into the garden, and if they are hardy they will return year after year.

*Lilies are very tall and slender, and therefore perfectly suited to be planted between other plants. If lilies are started early in pots, they can be placed outside, their flowers filling empty spots in flower beds.*

# WIDE BED SOWING FOR BOUNTIFUL FLOWER BEDS

Creating vibrantly colorful and rich flower beds and bouquets is one of the most rewarding aspects of gardening. Flowers can be direct-seeded into the flower beds for late-summer splendor, but for anyone looking to infuse their garden with a little . . . extra something, the greenhouse can help with handy shortcuts.

By sowing flowers in flats in the greenhouse you'll soon have small plants ready for the outside. Even diminutive plants that take their time in reaching the bloom stage will still flower earlier if started inside than if they're only direct-sown outside. They can be planted exactly where you want them, and also in the desired quantities.

Tall, late summer-flowering asters, together with snapdragons, painted daisies and brightly hued marigolds are but some of the flower options that delight the senses. Lately, many of the flower beds in public spaces have been planted with a handsome variety of different flowers. Some, like the annual royal knight's spur, require a long growth period before they flower; others, like nasturtiums, reach the flowering stage very quickly. But no matter what type of flowers you use, in order to achieve a dazzling display in your flower beds, all the flowers need to bloom simultaneously. While petunias are lovely to plant out and enjoy, if the nasturtium next to them won't bloom until later in the season, then a big part of the overall visual effect is lost. The possibility of starting plantings indoors to hasten the production of even the simplest plants is one of the great advantages of owning a greenhouse.

Some store-bought seeds certainly don't come cheap—that special kind of calendula, old-fashioned sweet pea or black nasturtium can set you back several dollars per seed packet. What's more, there's no guarantee that all seeds will emerge when they're direct-sown in the flower bed. Therefore, it's highly recommended to start these kinds of plants inside. Sowing seeds in a flat or a box increases your control over the end result—there's no risk of slugs or birds feasting on the fragile shoots, or that a sudden downpour will wash away the soil. The content of the seed packet is usually meager, especially if the seed is expensive, so in order to coax the most plants from the packet, the seeds should be sown in the greenhouse.

As it is such simple and quick work, it is no great bother to wide bed sow many of the garden's flowers. Besides, the plants are certain to grow in their assigned space once you manually plant them out. If you are planning to keep a vegetable patch edged by nasturtium, it would be quite irritating to see a bald spot because, for whatever reason, three seeds didn't take. It's also impossible to buy many of these plants as seedlings, at least of the rare varieties. An unusual white nasturtium or a creamy marigold, for example, makes for a delicate display along with a full-bodied grey violet opium poppy. By wide sowing in flats or boxes, you have the possibility of creating many of your own imaginative combinations in the garden.

*Preceding page: China (Annual) aster. Below: oriental poppy.*

*It's easy to wide sow Mexican Zinnias.*

# How to's—Wide sowing

◆ Fill shallow flats/boxes with planting soil. Use a mini-frame with a plastic lid if you have it. Fill the flats/boxes generously with commercial planting soil that is weed and disease-free.

◆ Pat down the soil firmly, paying special attention to the corners, and continue to add more soil until the flat/box is nearly full.

◆ Water with a watering can fitted with a fine nozzle; the soil should be soaked.

◆ Sow the desired seeds on the soaked soil, leaving ample space between each seed. Cover the seeds with soil according to the directions on the packet and lightly pat it down with the palm of your hand. The damp will rise up through the layer of soil.

◆ Place the flat/box directly in the greenhouse. Any plants that need higher temperatures for germination can stay inside the house until shoots appear. They can then be moved into the greenhouse as soon as they turn green.

◆ Water the seeded flat/box carefully, preferably using bottom-up irrigation if the flat/box has drainage holes at its base. If there are no holes, be extra careful when watering—don't water to the point where the flat/box becomes water-logged; in fact, water so sparingly that the flat/box nearly dries out. If you have sown in planting soil, start watering with liquid fertilizer when the shoots reach about 1 cm (1/3") high, and continue doing this. See p. 36.

## Transplanting outside

When the weather turns warm enough and the seedlings have reached 3 - 5 cm (1 1/4–2") high, it's time to move them into the garden. They can be used in many ways: in flower beds together with other flowers that needed an advanced start in-house; as fillers where a plant failed to grow or where the spring bulbs have started to fade;

or as colorful accents among late-flowering perennials. These kind of small plants are perfect for making beautiful combination plantings in large hanging baskets. They're also good for the vegetable patch, where their rows can provide cut flowers for bouquets. (Don't underestimate the thrill of having easy access to cut flowers for wonderful summertime hostess gift bouquets.) Many of the plants are also edible and make delicate garnishes for salads, drinks and cakes.

## Provisional flower beds

If you run out of containers and flower beds in which to put your plants, there is an easy fix: Cover the ground with a layer of newspaper and add an edging. (The edging can be made from a pallet collar, of wood or plastic, or untreated railway ties). Fill the space inside and along the edges up with store-bought, bagged planting soil mixed with some long-acting fertilizer. Insert the plants and wait for flowers to appear. These kinds of flower beds are good for areas where it's difficult to grow anything, such as areas under big trees or in front of a hedge. If the bed is set up under a tree or on a hard surface, it is advisable to put down a liner like a plastic cloth, root barrier, garbage bags or other material that will prevent water run-off.

*Next page: Wide bed sowing for the summer flower bed, and its outcome.*

### Suitable plants for wide bed sowing in flat/box

Snapdragon, *Antirrhinum majus*
Calendula, *Calendula officinalis*
China Aster, *Calistephus chinensis*
Painted Daisy, Tri-Color Daisy, *Chrysanthemum*
California Poppy, *Eschscholzia californica*
Sweet Pea, *Lathyrus odoratus*
Rose Mallow, *Lavatera trimestris*
Common Toad Flax, *Linaria maroccana*
Love-in-a-mist, *Nigella damascena*
Common (Opium) Poppy, *Papaver somniferum*
Clary Sage, *Salvia viridis*
Pincushion/Sweet Scabiosa, *Scabiosa atropupurea*
Signet Marigold, *Tagetes tenuifolia*
Indian Cress/Nasturnium, *Tropaeolum majus*
Canary Creeper/Nasturnium, *Tropaeolum peregrinum*
Mexican Zinnia, *Zinnia haageana*
Everlastings of different types, such as Sea lavender, Giant Strawflower, Paper Daisies and others, *Xerochrysum bracteatum*

# GROWING VEGETABLES IN THE GREENHOUSE

Vegetables are not only delicious and healthy for you; it's also great fun to pick a sun-ripened tomato bursting with flavor or a sweet, juicy cucumber right off the vine. While you can grow them outside, the greenhouse environment is a better bet because the harvest will be earlier and more bountiful.

You can follow all the rules to the letter when planting and growing vegetables, or you can make things a bit easier—but then your harvest might not be quite as abundant. There are many ways to go about growing vegetables, ranging from starting the plants from seed to buying mature plants in the garden center. If you'd like to start your plants from seed, check out chapter 4, page 29. Regardless of what growing method you pick, keep in mind that plants have basic requirements and will have to be grown in the greenhouse as they would be grown outside. The procedure described here is gleaned from professional growers' tips and tricks, which in turn have been adapted to ensure a comfortable atmosphere, all without having to resort to using harmful chemicals.

## Grow vertically

Most plants raised in a greenhouse are trained to grow vertically in order to maximize the use of all available space. Tomato, cucumber, melon and bell peppers can be trained with a long strand of twine that reaches all the way up to the ceiling. If you cultivate your crops vertically, the greenhouse becomes like a green arbor and all the plants will benefit from a good supply of light. You'll have a green jungle to sit and take delight in, as a tomato or cucumber plant can reach a height of more than 4 to 5 meters (13' to 16') during a single summer season. Bell peppers and eggplants don't grow quite as tall and lanky, so they can also be grown as bushes.

The plants can either be grown directly in the ground in the greenhouse, or can be potted in very large containers. While you can use a 10-liter (2.65 gallons) bucket, it's preferable to use larger pots—the soil tends to dry out more quickly in small pots and containers than in larger sizes. If the plant is potted, place a low growing plant in front of it to prevent the sun from shining directly onto the pot. Attach a nonslip loop of plastic string or twine to the base of the plant stem, being careful to not allow the loop to tighten around the plant and strangle it. Wind the twine around the stem of the plant upwards and towards its top. Move the twine past the plant top and fasten the straight twine tightly around a hook secured to the greenhouse structure. Use removable hooks that can be moved around without a problem—but they need to be the right type for greenhouse cultivation. The wrong kind of hook could become detached from the greenhouse, and make the whole plant collapse when weighed down by its fruit.

You can use common eyebolts for attaching the twine to the greenhouse if the structure is made of wood. Space the eyebolts out evenly—you'll need one for each plant. Instead of cutting off the twine once it reaches the greenhouse ceiling, leave a length of about 5 m (16') and loop it in a bundle and tie it together, or tie it securely around a support. Twice a week you'll add another loop of the twine around the growing stem to support the plant in its growth towards the top. The twine needs to be tight enough to provide adequate support for the plant, and long enough to support the whole plant during the entire season. As the plants grow taller they'll be moved sideways, step-by-step, by either moving the bolt/hook, or by simply moving all the support twine one step sideways in the same direction.

## Close but airy

Don't space the plants too closely together in the greenhouse. It's tempting to do so because the plants look quite tiny and spindly at the beginning, but it's necessary to follow proper spacing to prevent introducing or spreading disease. Always plant in a triangular pattern—in zigzag formation—in order to provide each plant with as much space as possible. This is something to remember even when dealing with potted plants. It's difficult to say just how much space is enough space between plants, but as a general guideline we use two to three tomato or cucumber plants, complete with access paths, per square meter (10.76 sq ft) of greenhouse surface. A 10 square meter (107.65 sq ft) greenhouse will hold approximately 25 big plants, in addition to a variety of potted plants. Grape vines and fruit trees need more room and thus will allow less space for other plant life.

*Vertical cultivating. The twine starts off attached to the base of the plant.*

*It is easier to grow tomatoes than to start tomato plants from seed.*

As the plants grow in height, you can plant lower-growing plants between them. Basil likes a lot of warmth and thrives in the greenhouse, especially between tomato and cucumber plants. While the plants grow, make sure to keep the soil below them clean and weed free. Even if there are other plants in between them, you'll need to keep the ground neat. Don't leave the weeds and clippings on the ground—they belong in the compost pile.

## Pruning

Many plants that grow in the greenhouse will need to be pruned. Not all shoots should be allowed to grow, as otherwise the greenhouse would turn into a dense, shadowy jungle where the plants would get insufficient light and space. Inferior and smaller fruits would hardly ripen, and plants might also abort their fruit—i.e., spontaneously shed their unripe fruit. Plants need sun and air to produce a good crop. (Each growing tip includes a proper pruning how-to related to the plant subject.)

Wilted and diseased leaves are cut off and thrown away. It's preferable that the leaves be kept off the ground to prevent the growth of grey mold. Leaves resting on the ground are cut off at the mere hint of trouble, so in the end the plant's bottom segment might look a little bare, but its upper part will be healthy and green. Most important is to make sure that the leaves at the top get plenty of light, as the bottom leaves quickly become spent and can subsequently be removed without a second thought.

## Do more companion planting

Even if you only buy plants, you might be lucky and happen upon several different varieties meant specifically for greenhouse growing. Take care to label your pots. Chili peppers come in different strengths; bell peppers in many beautiful colors; cucumbers vary in length; tomatoes might taste more or less sweet, even slightly tart, and they also vary widely in size and color. It isn't more challenging to grow several varieties, and it won't affect the quality of your harvest. It's perfectly fine to grow tomato and cucumber plants in the same greenhouse; just don't store their fruit together in the refrigerator.

## Tomatoes

Growing tomatoes in the greenhouse is both rewarding and easy. They do take a while to ripen, so if you'd like to enjoy tomatoes over the summer it's best to start the plants early. They can be started from seed indoors, or can be bought ready for transplanting at a nursery; the challenge lies principally in starting a tomato plant from scratch and not so much in growing the tomato itself. The advantage of starting the plant from seed is that you can select any type of plant you want; however, plants that you buy at a garden center are often of better quality than those started from seed at home, since they've been exposed to more light and the plant is more compact. Problems can arise in transporting the plant from the cultivator to the point of sale, which can stress the plants and make them not feel and look their best. They're also accustomed to the carefully maintained environment of a professional greenhouse, so they might have a rough time acclimatizing to a colder hobby greenhouse, and thus might slow down their rate of growth—at least initially. The hobbyist's own plants are already well used to less than ideal surroundings, and so have no reason to slow their growth in this manner.

From seed start to flowering stage, you can count seven to eight weeks under favorable conditions. Add another seven to eight weeks from bloom to ripe fruit. That adds up to almost four months, which means that if you want to eat tomatoes in July, you'll need to start your seeds in February.

*It's your choice: Start tomatoes from seed or buy young plants.*

## Selection

Tomatoes exist not just as different cultivars, but also in different types. Those that produce really small-sized fruit usually grow clusters containing lots of fruit. The bigger the tomato, the fewer tomatoes will be in the cluster. Mid-sized red varieties usually give the most fruit per kilo (around 2 lbs) weight per plant. The variety you choose to grow depends on your personal taste and preference, and flavors of tomatoes vary widely. Smaller tomatoes usually have a more pronounced, intense flavor, while big beefsteak, slicer-style tomatoes can be more subtle-tasting. It also depends on how they've being grown: plenty of sun and sparse (but not stingy) irrigation will help concentrate flavor in the fruit far better than if it's kept in a shady spot with plenty of water.

Seeds for good quality tomatoes are pricey—some can cost as much as ten to twenty Swedish Crowns ($1.50 to $3) per seed—but a good quality fruit is easier to grow than a cheaper variety. Good quality tomatoes also exhibit superior resistance to different diseases, and can tolerate vagaries in the weather without halting their growth. Seeds for many of the rare and quirkier kinds of fruit, such as the ancient heirloom varieties yielding black, green, stripy, pink, yellow and white fruits, are also available for sale on the market. These are often more unusual rather than of reputable quality, and expensive merely due to their rarity. The easiest fruit to cultivate are the red, regular-sized cultivars, quite simply because breeding programs have concentrated on producing this kind of uniform and reliable fruit. Also, as a rule, newer varieties tend to be more disease resistant. Nevertheless, it's always a good idea to grow several varieties of tomatoes for different uses: the common red greenhouse tomato for salads, a smaller variety to pick and eat straight from the plant, a yellow variety for its lovely color, and a tempting new cultivar. Grown together, they all make for a nice healthy mix.

## Care

A tomato plant is planted in a large pot, in a bag, or in the ground. It's trained to grow towards the ceiling as described earlier, on page 62. When flowers start to appear, give the plants a slight shake, or give them a quick shower, every day. Tomatoes are self-pollinating, but the pollen needs to fall onto the pistil for pollination to take place. When the plant is shaken or watered, the pollen loosens and then undertakes self-pollination. You need to water the plant daily—and drip irrigation is almost always a must. If you have not set up a drip irrigation system, you'll need to water the plant every morning, midday and early afternoon (but do not shower the plants in the evening, as this will gives disease an opportunity to set in). Count on giving a large tomato plant several liters (several quarts) of water each day. Do not use a hose or spray attachment when watering, as the water is too cold for the plant. Instead, collect water in drums and watering cans after the watering is done, then leave them in the

*The tomato plants are only transplanted into the ground when the soil is warm enough.*

*Shake or shower the plant so it can perform self-pollination.*

greenhouse until next watering. During that time the water will have time to reach a more gentle, lukewarm temperature.

Tomatoes prefer ambient temperatures around 20°C to 25°C (68°F to 77°F). Ventilate the surrounding air properly to keep the temperature constant and not too hot; an automatic roof ventilation system is very helpful (see page 146). Another way is to shower the floor to lower the temperature and raise the air's moisture content.

Remove sucker shoots and clean the tomato plant each week. Most greenhouse tomatoes are indeterminate, which means that they can reach dizzying heights. They grow sucker shoots in the joint where lateral stem meets the main stem, but they must be removed—these small shoots are called 'suckers' because they suck away nourishment and energy needed for the main plant. There might be shoots all the way down at the foot of the plant and they have to be removed as well. Even though the shoots are removed, you can be certain there will new ones the following week. Sucker removal is a chore that needs to be taken care of on a weekly basis, as there will always be new shoots sprouting, week after week. Everything wilted and dry must also be cleared away. The lower leaves will turn yellow after a while—cut off the most wilted ones, approximately three leaves per week—but don't remove all

bedraggled-looking leaves, as the plant needs green, working leaves in order to set fruit. Broken shoots, leaves and other damaged parts need to be removed. Keep winding the twine once around the plant's main stem each week (see page 62). Avoid wrapping leaves and flower clusters under the twine, as this can cause them to break off. The plant can be moved slightly to one side once it reaches the ceiling. The lower part of the plant—which will most likely be bare of leaves at this point—will lean away from its planting spot on the ground. If the plants are left to grow long enough, they will eventually 'walk' sideways around the greenhouse, like in next page's picture.

The tomato plant can continue to grow in this manner, with its uppermost segment always in the light, and continue to produce new flowers and fruit over a prolonged time period. If you'd rather not have such a big, tall plant, just top it off (in other words: cut the top off) when it reaches the ceiling. This will effectively stop any further setting of flowers.

Top off the plant once the summer comes to a close. As it takes about two months from flower to harvest, you can predict the approximate date at which you can do this, and which you'll need to do in order to divert the plant's energy into ripening its already existing green tomatoes.

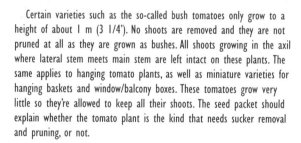

*When the plant reaches the ceiling, its top is moved sideways. This makes the plant lean.*

*Remove sucker shoots from the joint between lateral stem and main stem.*

Certain varieties such as the so-called bush tomatoes only grow to a height of about 1 m (3 1/4'). No shoots are removed and they are not pruned at all as they are grown as bushes. All shoots growing in the axil where lateral stem meets main stem are left intact on these plants. The same applies to hanging tomato plants, as well as miniature varieties for hanging baskets and window/balcony boxes. These tomatoes grow very little so they're allowed to keep all their shoots. The seed packet should explain whether the tomato plant is the kind that needs sucker removal and pruning, or not.

## The harvest

Check on the plant regularly, even if its irrigation and feeding are set up to take place automatically. Make sure it sets fruit, as each flower is a potential tomato in the making—big or small. Cherry tomatoes set many flowers so it's not quite as important that every flower be pollinated. The bigger the tomato, the fewer the flowers in the cluster, which means that it's much more important that they're all fruiting. The tomato starts out as a small, unripe, green fruit that grows and increases in size slowly. Usually, the tomatoes ripen one by one in the bunch, and they are harvested a few at a time. For grape tomatoes, the cluster is left intact until all fruits ripen

and the bunch becomes very heavy. At times you may have to use special plastic supports that you attach to the stem. You can often buy them at greenhouse supply stores and at seed firms catering to professional growers.

Pick your tomatoes regularly. If there are too many tomatoes on the vine at any time, it's better to pick them and keep them in the refrigerator than to leave ripe red ones on the plant. If the ripe fruit is left on the plant, then the plant will set flowers very sparingly, which in turn will make it produce less fruit in the long term.

Tomatoes can be frozen directly after picking, without blanching or cooking. Place them in a freezer plastic bag and, if you wish, add a few sprigs of fresh herbs (such as oregano and basil) to it. When you want to use the tomatoes, just add the herbs to them when you cook a sauce or a stew.

When the weather turns cold and it's time to empty the greenhouse, there will still be a lot of green unripe tomatoes left on the plants. Harvest them, either one by one or by bunches, leaving the blossom end and a piece of the stem intact, then let them ripen in a sunny spot in the house, or cook them while they're still green. To delay the ripening, and save the tomatoes as long as possible, store them in a cool place such as a pantry or root cellar.

*The greenhouse with loads of tomatoes at the height of summer. They ripen from the bottom up.*

### An array of tomato sizes

- *Cherry tomatoes: 10, 25, and 30 gr (1/2 oz., slightly under 1 oz., and slightly over 1 oz.)*
- *Plum tomatoes—larger and more elongated than cherry tomatoes: 30 to 50 gr (1 oz. to just under 2 oz.)*
- *Mid-sized tomatoes: 60 to 100 gr (just over 2 oz. to 3 1/2 oz.)*
- *Beefsteak tomatoes: a hefty 200 gr (around 7 oz.)*

## Problems

On the whole, growing tomatoes is easy: there are a few pests to contend with, but no major obstacles to overcome. There will always be some damaged and ruined fruit, especially during the fall. Much of the common damage is caused neither by disease, pests, or insecticide treatment.

Split fruit is usually caused by uneven irrigation and/or a sudden shift in temperature—a really hot August day followed by a chilly night, for instance. Split fruits is a common sight in the fall.

Curling at the edge of plant leaves is also caused by too large a temperature swing between night and day.

Leaf discoloration and yellowing tops are signs of nutrient deficiency, and which can be remedied by adding liquid fertilizer to the irrigation water. Even with automatic irrigation, it might be necessary to add extra nutrients to the water when plants are at their most productive.

Yellowing leaves at the bottom of the plant is a sign of natural aging. Simply snip them off, a few at a time.

If the plant sets no fruit even when there are flowers, the cause might be a lack of pollination. You'll need to jiggle, shake or shower the plant with a spray of water to help the pollen drop and reach the pistil. A beehive can be bought and placed in the greenhouse to promote pollination—they can be purchased from companies specializing in organic horticulture.

Lack of fruit can also be a sign of an overheated greenhouse. This is a very common problem. Tomatoes don't like temperatures above 25°C (77°F), and at 28°C to 30°C (82.4°F to 86°F) the flowers can no longer produce any fruit. Make sure to keep the greenhouse ventilated during the day, and leave doors and windows open if the greenhouse is going to be left without supervision over a few days during the summer. Refer to the part about ventilation on page 146.

Plants and fruit can be damaged by cold and frost during the fall. When clear or 'greasy' looking spots appear on the fruit, it's usually due to cold or frost damage. The green unripe fruit seems firm and unblemished but becomes soft and mushy when ripe.

## Pests

The tomato's main tormentors are usually *aphids* and *white flies*. Swedish cultivators use organic, eco-friendly treatments consisting of beneficial insects to combat pests, instead of using chemical insecticides. Organic methods work in hobby greenhouses, but they require constant temperature control. It can also get rather expensive for a hobby grower to buy these natural 'predators', but if you're interested in this method, refer to page 184 for suggested reading on this particular topic.

*Black soot* on the fruit flags a problem caused by aphids. The sticky ('honey dew') substance on leaves and on fruit is the telltale sign of an aphid infestation. A sooty fungus grows in the sticky substance, and while it's unsightly it is not dangerous, so just wash it off before eating the tomato. You can rid the plant of an aphid infestation by spraying it and the fruit with water, especially on the underside of the leaves. Plant sprays can also be used in several rounds, according to packet instructions.

Whiteflies, small and white, are also a form of aphid and they can be found on the leaves' underside. They can also cause Black soot. Spray with water and perhaps an organic pesticide. Unfortunately, whiteflies are difficult to get rid of—they move very quickly and the organic pesticide has to hit the whitefly directly in order to be effective.

*Vegetable hornworms* eat big holes in leaves and sometimes even in the fruit. They're difficult to get rid of, as they are busy movers. Pick off the visible ones, give the plants an early morning shake, then remove and destroy the larvae that fall to the ground.

*Slugs* make big holes, too. The difference here is that they secrete and leave a slimy, shiny trail behind them. Sneak into the greenhouse in the evening and try to collect them. You can also spread special slug bait that is harmless to other animals and to humans. This needs to be done at even intervals.

*Holly leaf miner* leaves behind long narrow winding trails. If there are only a few leaves that have been affected, simply remove and burn them; if the damage is more substantial there is nothing that can be done. You can stop an attack if you discover it early on, and if you remove the leaves at once. Still, the harvest will be smaller as some leaves have been destroyed.

## Fungal diseases

*Leaf mold* is a common problem during late summer and fall. This disease is common in both tomatoes and potatoes. Leaves on tomato and potato plants turn brown and wither. Cut away the affected leaves as soon as they show up, and throw them in the garbage or burn them. Don't grow potatoes beside or inside the greenhouse, and opt for varieties that are disease resistant—this will be highlighted on the seed package. Older tomato varieties featuring more potato-like leaves are more prone to this type of attack.

*Blossom-end rot* is a fungus that attacks the fruit. Tomatoes develop large dark spots that are firm at first, but then soften. The only thing to do is throw away the tomatoes that have been attacked. Blossom-end rot is common among fruits in the fall.

*Grey mold* is also a late summer problem. The leaves turn brown and are covered in grey fuzz. Cut off the leaves as soon as you see them, and remove them from the greenhouse. Avoid touching any greenery with the diseased leaves to prevent the spread of the spores to the rest of the greenhouse. A way to mitigate this problem is to heat the greenhouse during the night—a fan heater is good—and provide proper ventilation during the day. Grey mold thrives when the days are warm but the nights are cold and humid—a natural occurence in the fall. Don't irrigate or shower the plants in the afternoon, as the humidity stays on during the night.

*Powdery mildew* is another common fungal disease. It coats the plant in a white powdery substance. Some tomato cultivars are more susceptible to it than others. It's best to only grow disease-resistant varieties of tomatoes, because there isn't much that can be done once the plant has been attacked. If the fungus is discovered early, remove the affected leaves and spray the plant with an organic plant treatment. Try repeatedly spraying it with a garlic spray, as it has shown to help against powdery mildew on cucumbers.

*Bell peppers come in many colors.*

# Bell peppers and chili peppers

Bell peppers and chili peppers are fruits from the same plant. They're both Spanish peppers, and have been crossbred to produce the large, juicy, sweet and meaty fruits called bell peppers and the smaller pungent fruits with thin walls—the chili peppers. There are several kinds of peppers with edible fruits, of which the chili pepper is the most common. Both bell and chili peppers thrive in sunshine—the sunnier it is, the tastier the fruits will be.

Bell and chili peppers can both be bought as plants, or can be sown as seed. It's best to use commercial seeds when growing bell peppers, since the seeds in the bell pepper fruit from the vegetable bin at the grocery store rarely produce the same kind of fruit as the one that provided the seed; plus, it's not clear how long it will take to grow the pepper in the Swedish climate. It's better to buy a proven cultivar, either in a seed packet or as a plant, as that will guarantee the type that will grow to harvest in our climate. Chili peppers are a different story—it can feel a bit like an adventure to collect seeds from store-bought fruit. Just

keep in mind that the resulting fruit will not be exact copies of the original, and that the fruits will in all likelihood not taste the same. Seeds from fruits grown in Mexico but sold in Sweden will not grow into the same strong-tasting specimens.

## Care

Bell peppers and chili peppers can be grown in pots. Many varieties sold as seeds don't grow into large plants even if the fruits are large. You can grow them the same way as tomatoes, trained vertically with twine, and pruned heavily. Another way is to grow them wide and bushy in large pots. The large bush needs support in the form of a sturdy wooden stake—bell peppers especially, since the fruits can get heavy enough to break their stems. If the plant is grown as a bush, you won't need to remove any of the shoots.

Shape the trained plant by cutting off most of the shoots that sprout, and save one shoot to be trained vertically. Wrap the twine around the plant close to its planting spot, and fasten the twine to a hook or bolt in the ceiling. Remove the new shoots that appear at the top to keep only one main shoot. Two shoots often appear at the same time, so with time the plant gets a staggered look. You can also save two shoots further down on the plant—tie them to their separate pieces of twine, then lead those out from the plant and fasten them to the ceiling, which will give the plant the appearance of a Y. It's not as cumbersome as it sounds—the main thing is that the plant flowers and sets fruit, and that the sun gets a chance to shine on the plant.

## Harvest

Bell and chili peppers can be harvested both ripe and unripe. Depending on the variety, unripe ones start off green then ripen to yellow, red, orange, or blackish brown. There are others that are red when unripe only to turn into a brownish black color. The seed packet should provide this information so that it's clear when the time has come to harvest the fruit. There can be significant differences among the different varieties. While large fruits generally have a mild taste and smaller ones are stronger, this doesn't always hold true. There has been so much cross breeding that some fruits are reminiscent of tomatoes, while others are searing hot. The heat strength of the fruit should be labeled on the seed packet. Most commonly, unripe fruits are milder tasting than ripe ones.

While the fruit is ripening and still attached to the plant, flower production slows down. You'll have a bigger harvest—i.e., more bell and chili peppers per plant—if the fruit is picked unripe. Snip off the fruit, leaving a piece of the stem attached. If the stem is removed, it leaves a hole in the fruit that can start to rot, shrivel up, or go moldy. Bell peppers can be harvested a few

*Ripe, burning hot red pepper.*

at a time and frozen. They are not good candidates for ripening inside, as the fruit will shrivel up.

Harvesting pepper fruits requires extra caution, because the fruit can be very hot, so if you touch your face or rub your eyes after holding a pepper, it might make your face and/or eyes burn for quite a while. Peppers don't ripen once they're picked, but they can be dried; leave them sitting longer on the plant, then dry them in a sunny spot with good air circulation. You can also thread the peppers on a coarse thread and hang them out in the sun to dry. Do not leave the peppers in a pile, or they risk going moldy.

## Problems
Yellowing leaves can plague both bell and chili pepper plants. The reason might be that they have dried out too much, or that they suffer from a lack of nitrogen. Try adding liquid fertilizer to the irrigation, then check to see if new emerging shoots are green. The leaves can also turn yellow or lilac, or show yellow spotting when nighttime temperatures dip, which is something these plants don't like at all. Unripe fruit that falls off the plant can be a sign that it lacks water and/or nutrients (as there are often many fruits developing at the same time) so make sure the plant receives weak fertilizer each time it is watered.

If you see brown, spotty, shriveled, and malformed fruits, or notice that some fruits don't grow as well as others, you can always remove them from the plant since it's counterproductive to make the plant expend energy on developing fruits that are going to end up being inferior to the rest. However, fruits that are merely disfigured due to an insect's bite or sting taste just as good as unblemished fruit, so they can be put to use in a salad or hidden in some other dish.

## Pests
Both bell and chili peppers suffer from frequent infestations of *aphids* and *whiteflies*, which are a form of lice that spread rapidly and are extremely frustrating to deal with. To make the task of keeping the infestation under control a little easier, place the plants outside when it's warm and shower them. While it's practically impossible to eradicate all the aphids and whiteflies, you can spray the plant with organic insecticides—but not under direct sun, as this will cause the leaves to burn. The advantage of growing plants in pots is that the affected plant can be moved out of the greenhouse, thus ensuring that the other plants in the greenhouse are not affected to the same degree. Check the underside of leaves often to catch when the onslaught begins (the emphasis here is not on *if*, but on *when*), as it will be easier to treat the problem successfully the sooner it's discovered.

*Spider mites* will occasionally attack bell and chili peppers. They show up as teeny tiny yellow spots on the leaves (see the example of a cucumber plant, page 76).

*Slugs* will eat the leaves, so spread special slug bait, then pick up and dispose of all signs of slugs.

## Fungal diseases
*Grey mold* and other fungal diseases can show up in late summer and in the fall. Remove shriveled, brown leaves with greyish fuzz as soon as they appear; be careful not to shake them around in the greenhouse, and wash your hands and the tools used to remove the grey mold, because grey mold spores are small and spread easily. Leaves should be dug down in the compost pile or thrown directly in the trash bin.

*The eggplant flower illustrates that the plant is a close relative of the potato.*

# Eggplant

The eggplant is also a relative of the tomato and thus likes warmth and sun. If it hasn't been started in the greenhouse in the spring, it will not have adequate time to produce a crop. When the summer warms up it can be placed outside, just like bell and chili peppers, but it does need a longer stretch of summer climate than is typical for Sweden. Eggplants can be trained to grow vertically with the help of twine, but most common varieties are low and bushy. They produce fruits that are slightly smaller in size than the dark purple, pound-sized fruits we find in the vegetable aisle at the grocery store. The fruits come in white, lilac, green or stripes, they are oblong or round, or small and fingerlike. The smaller, finger-like type is favored in Asia, while Southern Europe is partial to the rounder, purple variety.

If you want to grow your preferred kind of eggplant, you'll have to start the plants from seed. Eggplant seeds are not a common sight in garden centers, although they do exist. Buy your seed in packets—do not attempt to use seeds from fruits. Also, seeds bought during a holiday trip to a warmer climate will require a far longer and warmer summer than we typically have in order to produce food that is edible; you will have far better success if you purchase your seed from Swedish producers that carry seeds best suited to Sweden's northern climate.

## Care

Sow each seed early and in its own pot, and place them in a spot with plenty of light. They need 25°C to 30°C (77°F to 86°F) to germinate, and require a long growth period inside. Pot them up into larger containers several times, and don't move them into the greenhouse until it's warm in there both day and night—these plants demand high soil temperature. Use some caution while irrigating the plants during the seedling stage—let the soil dry out slightly between waterings.

Later, place the plant—whether seeded or bought—in a large pot and fertilize regularly. If the plant is to be trained vertically, remove all the shoots except for one or two, and attach them with twine to hooks or eyebolts in the ceiling structure. The twine follows the plant and is looped around it as it continues to grow.

When the plant starts to flower, help it along by patting it softly inside the flower with a small watercolor paintbrush to ensure that pollination occurs. This might not be entirely necessary, but do it anyway—better to be safe than sorry. If you want to grow your plant into a bush-like shape, top five or six leaves to make it branch out well.

## Harvest

Eggplants will fruit without pollination, but require warm days—preferably around 25°C (77°F)—and cooler nights, for this to take place. Pick the fruits as they ripen and are of the right size and color. The quickest fruit to grow are the small varieties that have their origins in Asia. Don't leave the fruits on the plants longer than necessary—pick them and store them in the refrigerator instead. The eggplant will not ripen after being picked, and should either be used directly or stored in a cool place.

## Problems

Yellow or discolored leaves may be caused by chilly nights, since eggplants need warmth to thrive.

Plants that refuse to grow are probably in soil that's too low in temperature—they will stop growing completely if placed in cold soil. Low soil temperature and/or lack of nutrients will also cause the plant to shed its fruit.

*Eggplants can have white, green, or lilac skins, and come in different sizes.*

## Pests

*Aphids* and *whiteflies* are common problems. The leaves of the eggplant are slightly fuzzy, which makes for a comfortable, protected space for the aphids, and by the same token makes it challenging to dislodge them by showering the plant—which is more easily done on the bell and chili peppers' shiny, slick leaves. Check the underside of the eggplant leaves at even intervals to try and spot the aphids as early as possible. Shower the plants with water and spray with organic pest control as needed. Move heavily infested plants outside, away from the rest of the plants.

Spider mites produce light spots on the slightly fuzzy leaves of eggplant. It's a pretty common problem (see an example on a cucumber on page 76).

## Fungal diseases

Eggplant risks being affected by *grey mold* if the atmosphere turns cold and damp. There's no remedy except proper ventilation in the greenhouse during the day, and the use of a fan heater during the night.

If the plants have been kept outside during part of the summer they will need to move into the greenhouse at night once the evenings turn chilly and damp again.

## Pepino (Solanum muricatum)

A pepino looks similar to an eggplant. It has a bush-like growing habit with many branches. Its flowers shift from white to blue violet, and after a while it produces oval greenish-white fruits with stripes in brownish lilac. The plants grow very rapidly and require heavy fertilizing to bloom and produce fruit, but the plant itself doesn't grow taller than approximately one meter (3' 1/4).

You can buy pepino seeds, but it's more common to buy the plant itself. You'll seldom find more than one variety of pepino in Sweden, as this is an unusual vegetable for the country—both in seed and plant form. Pepino is grown like an eggplant, is an excellent potted plant for the greenhouse, and needs warmth to thrive. The fruits grow fast after pollination; they have a sweet melon-like taste and are eaten fresh without any special preparation.

# Cucumber

Cucumbers are as easy to grow as tomatoes. Cucumber plants yield more quickly; there is less wait time between sowing and harvesting. Small cucumbers are sweet and tasty even if they're picked a bit too early, while early unripe tomatoes are not tempting. Cucumbers require more heat than tomatoes, and are even more chill sensitive.

It's easy to start cucumber plants, but the cost of quality seeds can be steep. A seed packet will often contain only five seeds, and among those only four will germinate. For this reason, each seed deserves its own container. Make sure to choose a variety of garden cucumber especially bred for greenhouse cultivation. A combination of parthenocarpic and gynoecious varieties is best, as they contain mostly female flowers that require no pollination; these are also good if you want to avoid pesky cucumber seeds. There are traditional, long cucumbers, as well as newer, shorter varieties—the greenhouse mini cucumbers. Both are smooth skinned and dark green. Powdery mildew affects cucumbers easily, so make sure that the varieties you choose are powdery mildew resistant. This information should be printed on the seed packet.

Cucumber plants age much quicker than tomato plants, so it's a good idea to save a few seeds for planting later on in the season. Depending on where you live and the date for first frost for the area, it might be worth the effort to put a few new sturdy plants in the greenhouse in July. Sow directly into pots and place them in the greenhouse, ready at hand when needed.

## Care

The temperature needs to reach 25°C to 28°C (77°F to 82.5°F) in order for cucumber seeds to germinate. Place the seeded pots on a tray on a windowsill above a radiator. Cucumbers don't transplant gladly from flat to pot, so it's better to direct sow one seed into each pot. After a few weeks the plant will be big enough to be safely moved into the greenhouse. Don't make this move too early, however, as the cucumber won't tolerate below 15°C (59°F) temperature during the night. If it's too cold, the plant can stop growing and will simply turn yellow. Store-bought cucumber plants will often stop growing momentarily when they are moved from a well-heated commercial space to a hobby greenhouse, but after a few weeks they usually begin to grow again. The plant grown from seed at home should spend a few weeks in the greenhouse before being planted out.

Cucumbers grow quickly in a warm environment, so the timeframe from sowing to harvest depends mostly on the weather. It can happen quickly if there is a heat wave at onset of June. If spring is cold, however, the plants may sulk and nothing may happen for several weeks. That's why growing times can't ever be exact—there can only be approximations. Once the plant starts to grow, it can develop 10

cm (4") in a single day, so you'll need to work fast to get the plant in the ground, train it and tie it up before it gets so long that it breaks.

If you're growing cucumbers in large containers, place them on a bottom layer of soil in the reserved pots and fill with warm soil, not with soil from bags (which can be too cool). If the plant is to go directly in the ground, don't dig a deep hole. Simply place it on the broken surface and then fill the hole and surround it with store-bought soil. It will end up looking somewhat like a small hillock. It's probably still a bit cold in the ground even though the surface may be warm; you can measure the soil's temperature with a special thermometer before planting the cucumbers to make sure that it's at the desired temperature—about 15°C (59°F).

Cucumber plants have frail roots and delicate stems. The roots don't have the strength to draw up enough water to sustain the whole plant. It's not unusual to see plants droop during the hottest part of the day. Left in this condition, neither plants nor fruit will grow, so shower the plants several times a day when the weather is warm and sunny. If you haven't set up a drip irrigation system, you'll need to water the plants several times a day, avoiding late afternoons and evenings—humidity and dampness late in the day increases the risk of the plant developing grey mold.

## Pinching and pruning

A thriving cucumber grows almost like a weed. Small shoots and budding, immature fruit grow together at the leaf axils. Pinch off the shoots without damaging the immature fruit. Each budding fruit consists of a small yellow flower attached to a swollen 'body' that will eventually develop into a cucumber.

Cucumbers are trained with twine attached to the ceiling, just like tomatoes (see pages 62 and 66), and are moved sideways in the same manner when they reach the ceiling. Another method is to pinch off the top, and leave two shoots in the leaf axil to develop into two new tops that are allowed to hang, or grow downwards. Depending on individual preference and available space, the new tops can also be allowed to grow sideways along the ceiling.

Alternatively, you can save a shoot from the plant early on and train it sideways. This will make the plant form a big Y with two lengths of twine from the base of the stem and up to the ceiling. That way, two cucumber plants will grow from one quality plant (if they're expensive), or if one has broken off, wilted or has died down.

The best way to heal a damaged stem is to dab some soil on the wound. Wilted, yellowing leaves are of no use, and should be cut off.

*Flower and immature cucumber show clearly here. Small shoots that need to be pinched off grow in the same space.*

*Showering the plants reduces the risk of spider mites.*

*Immature fruit, and a soon ready-to-harvest cucumber.*

## Harvest

Cucumbers grow from the plant stem and need to hang unobstructed—immature fruit can't be trapped in the supporting twine. The first cucumbers will appear at the bottom of the plant and then progressively higher up. It's important to keep pinching the top to encourage the plant to grow, to produce more leaves and new fruit in the axils. Cucumbers can be harvested at any stage, even when they are tiny; the little ones are delicious, but harvesting early means that the yield in kg (lbs) per plant will be lower than if the fruit were left to ripen longer. The best time to pick them is when the fruits are the size of commercially sold cucumbers.

Don't let cucumbers grow too large, and don't leave them sitting on the plant. Extra large cucumbers are not the mark of a master gardener—quite the contrary: large, pale green cucumbers are not tasty, and they hinder the plant from setting new fruit. A cucumber with only one swollen end should be harvested immediately, as it has only been partially pollinated and will never improve. You should eat it, however, as it's delicious while still small. It's not uncommon for a plant to set more immature fruit than will reach full maturity. If there are yellowing or withered immature fruits, remove them to leave the plant more energy for the remaining maturing cucumbers.

## Problems

Many problems suffered by cucumbers are caused by lack of heat. Yellowing plants, plants that stop growing—these are examples of problems that are caused by chilly nights. Leaves that turn yellow while the plant is still young is yet another cold environment issue, and might be the reason for yellowing fruit that drops off the plant. When plants won't grow, cold is usually the culprit. Irrigation and fertilizing is highly important, as yellowing leaves and falling fruit might also be caused by lack of nutrients and water.

## Pests

*Spider mites* (also simply called mites) are cucumbers' biggest enemy. At first, the leaves show yellow spots before turning dusty grey, after which they wilt and die. The whole plant is affected—it becomes weak and yields little, as it depends on green leaves for energy to continue to grow. Treat it by showering the plant inside the greenhouse during the middle of the day, when the atmosphere is at its warmest and driest. Automatic fogging or misting (see page 167) is a good solution. Remove all yellow leaves immediately, and spray regularly with organic, non-toxic plant treatments. Swap out your severely mite-bitten plants for new, healthy ones. Clean the

*Growing cucumber plants. They don't take long to go from flower to mature and ready to pick.*

greenhouse thoroughly each fall, as spider mites will often overwinter in the greenhouse, and are ready to infect new young plants in the spring.

Aphids like cucumbers, but they too can be fought with organic treatments. Cucumber leaves are slightly sticky, which gives aphids a good grip and protection, so make sure to spray the underside of the leaves extra carefully. Irregularly formed cucumbers can be the result of an infestation of the *tarnished plant bug (lygus lineolaris)*. This pest injects the fruit with a poison that terminates all growth in that spot, which usually causes some malformation in the fruit. The fruits are perfectly all right to pick, as they are still edible—their growth pattern has changed but they are neither poisonous nor dangerous.

## Fungal diseases

*Powdery mildew* can attack cucumbers. Entire leaves can look as though they've been dipped in a milky liquid; sometimes it's white and powdery. Buy only disease resistant plant varieties, and maybe spray with organic, nontoxic plant treatments, or treatments containing garlic extract. Weed meticulously between the plants and remove all plant leaves that touch the soil.

*Gummy stem blight* rots the narrow end of the cucumber. Be extra careful to keep the soil area clean around the plants, and clean by removing all plant debris and affected parts. Air out the greenhouse during the day to prevent high levels of nighttime humidity.

*Grey mold* makes cucumbers turn brown, tapering off to grey fuzz. Leaves and stems can also be affected. It's easy to recognize the grey fuzz, as it also regularly appears on strawberries. If the plant is young, you can try to remove the infected part as part of the cure, and then patch the bare spot with soil. If the attack occurs during late summer or fall, you may as well remove the affected part and hope for the best. Cold, wet nights are the culprit, and the way to combat this is, again, to air out the greenhouse properly during the day and use a fan heater during the night to prevent moisture build-up.

# Melons

Melons look a lot like cucumbers, but they usually only yield a few fruits per plant, as they are so much larger. Our selection of melon types is rather slim in seed packets, because Sweden is just a tad too chilly for them, and they almost always need to be grown in a greenhouse. We do have a smaller muskmelon variety, Aroma, that has been melon growers' to-go fruit for many years. 'Sweetheart' is also easy to grow, is self-pollinating, and produces many small fruits. Varieties offered by foreign seed companies can be problematic to grow here, as they usually require much more warmth over a much longer time span than Sweden has to offer. A truncated growing season will bear melons that lack their characteristic sweetness and taste. You may succeed, however, if the summer is warm and sunny.

## Care

Melons are sown and cared for in the same manner as cucumbers. It'll take between four and six weeks between sowing and transplanting them to the greenhouse. Melons can be grown in-ground or in large containers; they need very warm soil—nothing below 20°C (68°F). The plants are trained in the same way as cucumbers, with the help of twine that is fastened to the ceiling. The twine is attached around the plant stem at soil level, but the fruits will require added support: each individual fruit needs to be supported separately by mesh bags (or netting) that are fastened to eyebolts attached to the greenhouse structure. If not, the heavy fruit will dislodge the whole plant; if the plant tumbles to the ground the stem will break, and the fruit will burst. The string might also break. Raffia ribbon is not strong enough here, so use plastic covered parcel string instead.

## Pinching and pruning

Melons are pruned according to cultivar. Slow-growing varieties with closely spaced leaves are topped over three leaves, leaving two shoots to grow towards the ceiling, just like the cucumber plants. The old variety called 'west' (which is still sold in the garden centers) is such a melon. The sturdier and faster growing varieties, with wider spacing between leaves, are trained while the tops are left intact.

Pinch off the side shoots that appear in the leaf axils and are missing female flowers. Side shoots with female flowers are removed one leaf from the flower/fruit. If additional shoots appear on the new leaves' axils, repeat by removing shoots outside one leaf (this may seem like a bit of a chore, but it really isn't labor-intensive). What remains is a trained vine that reaches the ceiling. A shoot with an immature fruit should stay in each leaf axil, or no shoot at all. Any excess shoots with immature fruit are removed, as each plant can only support so many fruits.

## Pollination

In order to ensure a decent harvest, melons need help with pollination. Pollinate several flowers in one go while they're in bloom. If they are all pollinated at the same time, they will grow evenly and will likely be of similar size. (If the pollination is out of sync, the first ripe melons might become much larger, to the detriment of the later ones.) Use a small make-up or watercolor brush; start by dipping the brush carefully in the male flower, then pat the collected pollen on to the female flower. The female flower is the one with a 'rounder' profile, due to a slight swelling below the petal tube. For successful pollination, the ambient temperature must be above 18°C (64.5°F), and the best time to do this is before midday.

You can leave two or three melons on a vine to grow and ripen. Other immature fruit should be removed, but it will totally depend on the variety of the fruit. Its size can reach 1/2 to 2 kg (1 to 4.5 lbs). The description on the seed packet should state what kind of melon it is and how large the fruits are expected to grow. If all the fruits are left on the vine to mature, it will yield many melons but the fruit will be small. Let the melon grow over the summer, and make sure it gets plenty of water and nutrients.

# Watermelon

Watermelon is not of the same species as our most familiar melons, and it is a different plant. Its fruits are much larger and heavier - between 1.5 and 3 kg (3 and 7 lbs). They are suitable for growing lying prone on the ground.

There is a slightly smaller watermelon variety, 'sugar baby,' which has yellow flesh. It's well worth trying to grow, as it doesn't reach the size of the other, larger types. Place a stone, a piece of Masonite board or something similar under the fruit to protect it from the ground, otherwise the rind might rot if it's in direct contact with the soil.

Melons, both the more familiar varieties as well as the watermelons, can also be grown in cold frames. As they require a relatively large space to grow compared to their fruit yield, it's an efficient way to free up room in the greenhouse for other plantings. Start the plants in large pots in the greenhouse, and don't transplant them into cold frames until the summer heat is truly upon you. Be particular in removing wilted and dead leaves and in making sure the plant environment is kept clean.

## Harvest

Melons should be harvested once the fruit is ripe. This means that they should smell like melons, and that a soft indentation can be made at the stem: put a thumb on each side of the stem and press lightly; there should be a slight 'give' on the surface (this sounds easier than it actually is, especially if you're unused to performing

*Melons yield few but large fruits. The heavy fruit needs individual mesh or net support.*

this test.) The time it takes from pollination to ripe fruit is approximately twelve to fourteen weeks, depending on variety. The fruits can probably ripen a little more at room temperature once they've been picked, but they should not be harvested if they're too unripe. Remove all yellowed and misshapen fruit from the vine immediately, as they will never improve and are only siphoning away nutrients from the good ripening fruit.

## Problems

Melons experience the same problems as their close relative the cucumber—they're both very sensitive to chill and high humidity during the nighttime. Most of their issues stem from too low temperature, but melons are even more sensitive to cold than cucumbers, plus they require pollination. The absence of fruit might be caused by non-pollination, as female flowers need temperatures of at least 18°C (64.5°F) for pollination to take place. If there are only male flowers on the vine, then female flowers have failed to form due to the cold.

## Pests

*Spider mites* are a problem for melons. Their leaves become spotty, dry up, and drop (see the example of a cucumber, on page 76).

*Slugs* favor damp leaves that grow close together. They chew large holes in the leaves and can move high up into the plants. Trails of glistening slime are their giveaway, so search for them in the morning and evening damp, and get rid of them—this is especially important if the plants are trailing on the ground. Make a slug trap from an upside-down pot containing a potato sliced in half; reset the trap regularly. A beer trap placed among the leaves is another effective slug bait. Occasionally during hot summer days, larger animals such as frogs, hedgehogs, and cats seek out the cool and the shade that the lush greenery provides along the ground, but they won't damage anything and are not harmed by slug bait.

## Fungal diseases

The many leaves and their close proximity to each other makes for plenty of humidity around the plants. Since they're extremely sensitive to drought and have frail root systems, you'll need to water them often. This, however, makes for an ideal environment in which *grey mold* can move in and feel right at home. Remove the parts of the plant affected by this mold, and keep the area clean and airy by not setting the plants too closely to each other, and by avoiding irrigating them in the evenings. Another possible solution to this issue is to preemptively spray the plants with organic, nontoxic anti-fungal protection.

*Ground cherry looks a lot like Japanese Lanterns. They have the same husk, but in different colors.*

# Cape gooseberry, ground cherry, and tomatillo

Cape gooseberry, ground cherry and tomatillo are all from the genus *physalis* and are close relatives of the garden plant bladder cherry—also known as 'Japanese lantern'. All of them bear fruits covered by a paper-like husk. The Japanese lantern husk is large and beautifully colored in orange, but the fruit itself is small. Ground cherry and cape gooseberry have larger fruit and their papery husk is a simple, plain brown protection.

Ground cherry and cape gooseberry are very similar, and their sweet-sour taste is akin to that of the tomato. These berries can often be found in the produce section of the grocery store, packaged in small clamshell containers, but they're also very easy to grow at home.

The tomatillo is a pale green-white fruit that fills its papery husk until it outgrows the husk and bursts out of it. The fruit itself is as large as a plum tomato, but remains light green as it ripens. One of its most common uses is in salsa verde, a condiment typical of Mexican cooking. The tomatillo tastes like a blend of kiwi fruit, melon and tomato. Cape gooseberry and ground cherry are easily found at the grocery store, and

*Ground cherry with its papery husk.*

*Tomatillos are attractive and very tasty. They look like ground cherry but are as large as golf balls.*

are available as plants or as seeds for starting your own plants, although there's usually little variety to pick from. Tomatillo is less common in Sweden and is not easy to find as a plant, so you will need to grow it from seed.

## Care

Ground cherry, cape gooseberry and tomatillo are simple to grow, but they need a long summer. It's advisable to start them out in the greenhouse before moving the plants outside during high summer. Bought or seed-started plants can be planted in large pots or in-ground in the greenhouse, where they'll grow into sturdy bushes that thrive in the sun and heat. Water regularly, fertilize, and keep the area clean around the plants. Once outside, they need to be in the sunshine with some protection from weather and wind.

## Harvest

The fruits are harvested one by one as they ripen—you'll need to taste a few to determine if they're ready to pick. Cape gooseberry and ground cherry should be a fairly intense shade of orange, and tomatillo will be light greenish white and have a slightly sweet taste; its husk will have split and curled away completely from the outgrown fruit. The fruits drop easily, so it's best to harvest them often, or they'll be lost on the ground. Cape gooseberry and ground cherry keep well and will continue to ripen after harvest—they can be stored for several weeks in a cool place. The larger tomatillo is not as good a keeper, but can still ripen a little after harvesting.

## Problems

Though all these plants are easy to grow, they can still develop yellowing leaves. The cold, a lack of nutrients or water can be culprits. These plants need a lot of sun and heat—a cold, rainy summer will make them unhappy and yield few fruits.

## Pests

*Whiteflies* are always an issue around these kinds of thin-leaved plants that are irrigated frequently. Check both the tops and undersides of leaves regularly after an infestation. Organic pesticide can be useful after an attack; if the plants are in containers, move them out of the greenhouse before the pests can get to other plants.

*Slugs* can also be a problem. Collect the slugs and spread slug bait regularly.

## Fungal diseases

Leaves can wither and be attacked by *grey mold*. Remove the affected leaves immediately and throw them in the garbage. Make sure the plants are spaced well enough apart from each other, as they grow close and grow many leaves. Remove wilted leaves, other plant debris, and keep the plant tidy.

# VEGETABLES TO PLANT OUTSIDE

Growing vegetables has often been considered a chore—a bit dull, yet necessary. Nowadays, few of us grow vegetables for survival as in years past; we choose instead to grow foods with health and wellbeing in mind.

Fresh and newly harvested vegetables are an integral part of a high quality of life. A greenhouse gives us the opportunity to start plants from seed, which are then easier to cultivate and to make more efficient use of the space in the greenhouse. It also helps curtail the need for extensive weeding, and promotes an earlier and more productive harvest.

The best way to avoid weeding is to start seeds, and then plant the seedlings outside when they're ready. If you've let your designated plot get overgrown with weeds—perhaps more than once—just remove them all before setting out the vegetable plants. It can sometimes be hard to tell a weed from a seedling, and then to weed between the plants, but you can take guesswork out of it altogether if the plants are put into a freshly weeded plot.

Start in early spring by working up the vegetable garden. Weed seeds and mature weeds are already in the ground, and they usually turn green long before the cultivated plants do. Raking the soil thoroughly will bring more seeds to the surface where they then will germinate; they can be removed a week or so later. If the soil is dry, watering can coax more seeds to germinate. Once the weeds are green, walk with a long-handle or draw hoe over the whole surface and weed. Do this on a sunny day, and leave the weeds out to dry up until the next day. You'll need to repeat this routine once or twice. A roto-tiller can also be used to clean the soil's surface. Meanwhile, your plants will be waiting and growing inside the greenhouse.

## Plant cell trays

Plant cell trays are convenient because the seedlings don't need to be potted up after being sown. They get a proper start, and there's no need to tear up and disturb their roots. The cells are placed directly in the vegetable plot and the young plants can continue to grow unimpeded. They also leave room for many more plants to grow than if each were in its own individual pot, and they take up fewer resources. The seeds germinate and grow more evenly in warmed soil in the greenhouse than in the ground. More seeds germinate and their growth is stronger because they get a quicker head start.

The main inconvenience of cell trays is that the plants can't be left too long in the cells. There's only room for a small amount of soil, so the young plants can quickly become root-bound if they're not planted out in time. When this happens their growth comes to a stop, and they experience difficulty growing properly once they are planted out.

*Cell tray growing produces many plants for planting out. Here are different kinds of lettuce.*

*Beans need warm soil. They get this in the greenhouse when planted in cell trays with big holes.*

*To save space, corn is started in cell trays before being potted up.*

### Vegetables that can be started in cell trays

Onions, *Allium cepa*

Scallions, (Spring onions), *Allium fistulosum*

Leeks, *Allium porrum*

Dill, *Anethum groveolens*

Chard, *Beta vulgaris*

Cauliflower, *Brassica*

Broccoli, *Brassica*

Brussels sprouts, *Brassica*

Red cabbage, *Brassica*

Spring (Early) cabbage, *Brassica*

White cabbage, *Brassica*

Mizuna (Japanese mustard) cabbage, *Brassica*

arugula, *Eruca*

Lettuce, *Lactuca*

Parsley, *Petroselinum crispum*

Beans, *Phaseolus vulgaris*

Peas, *Pisum sativum*

Spinach, *Spinacia oleracea*

# How to's—Vegetable cultivation

◆ Vegetable plants can be started very simply from seed by using cell trays or flat trays. They look like large plastic trays with plenty of small perforations at the bottom. These small holes, also called cells, are filled with soil that is packed down firmly.

◆ Water the surface thoroughly.

◆ Plant a few seeds in each cell, and cover according to packet instructions.

◆ Keep the cell tray in a place at room temperature. It doesn't need to be exposed to light until the surface shows sign of green; then it needs to be moved into the light immediately. Sowing is usually done in the house or in the greenhouse—the greenhouse being preferable, as filling the trays up with soil can be a messy job.

◆ Once the seeds have germinated, clip or pinch off plants in order to leave just one shoot in each cell.

◆ Let the seedlings grow for two to three weeks, depending on the type of plant. They'll be ready to transplant once the roots are big enough to keep the whole cell—soil and all—together so that it can be moved in one piece.

◆ Once the seedlings have emerged from the soil in the cells, you'll need to add weak fertilizer each time you water them, because planting soil contains no nutrients. The best way to do this is to place the cell tray into a plastic tray and add water directly into the plastic tray; this will let the soil draw up the water and fertilizer from underneath.

◆ Many cell trays come in a complete kit (root trainers) with cells, reservoir pan and holder for easy removal. If there isn't a holder, use a small, blunt wooden pin instead.

◆ Never pull out or yank on the plant. Put the seed cell on its side, and use your fingers to gently nudge the plant out of the cell if it's stuck.

## Planting

When the plants reach a few centimeters (about an inch) high, it's time to plant them out. They'll need to be hardened off for a week or two before transplanting, so move them outdoors in the morning and then bring them back inside at night, during their last week in the greenhouse. When planting them outside, you can amend the soil around each plant by adding some long-acting fertilizer, if needed. A small indentation around each plant will help with irrigation—use a watering can without a spray nozzle, and gently aim water at this indentation around each plant. Water the plant even if the soil is already wet so it can close up around the root clump. The root clump should not be exposed above the soil surface, or it will dry out very quickly.

*Above: Seed directly in the cell. Above right: There are many kinds of cell trays. Middle: The cells are emptied out with the help of pop-out brims. Below: The roots and soil should hold together in the cell that is ready to be transplanted.*

When all plants are in place and watered, cover them with a fiber cloth row cover (placed over metal hoops) to ensure an even better outcome. The cover emits warmth during the night, and protects the plants against strong sun during the day. The plants will acclimatize quicker to their new environment if the cover is left on, and it also protects them against attacks from cabbage moths and other flying insects—but only if it's left on during the greater part of the summer. Alternative housing for the plants is in a cold frame (see chapter 10, page 92). The cells can also be planted in the ground inside the greenhouse to provide an extra early harvest of tender springtime vegetables.

## Root vegetables

Carrots and beets—vegetables grown for their edible, tasty roots—can also be started in cell trays. In fact, they should not be started in normal pots, as their roots will be damaged when the small plants get potted up. However, the root in the cell can continue to grow undisturbed after transplanting— the trick is to pack the soil just right. The soil needs to stay together but can't be packed so tightly that the roots can't penetrate, so planting these vegetables takes a bit of practice. Here it's critical to have only one plant in each cell. If you see several seedlings, use a pair of nail scissors to avoid damaging the roots, and carefully cut away all plants except one. It's not worth your time and effort to start radishes from seed, as they are such fast growers.

## Herbs

Parsley, chives and dill are examples of herbs that are frequently used in Swedish food, but it can be tricky to get their seeds to germinate. Dill needs warmth and is very susceptible to root rot; it's good to sow dill in cell trays and then transplant it outside in a warm and sheltered spot.

Parsley is often in competition with weeds, and it's challenging to weed it since you can hardly see the row of parsley, as it's a very slow grower. You can dodge this problem by sowing parsley in cell trays. Another benefit to starting herbs this way is when a sown plant must stand a while longer before it can be transplanted out: the smaller the space it takes up, the better.

Even perennial herbs can be sown in cell trays to facilitate planting out. Salvia, thyme and rosemary, for example, can be seed started and are not very demanding when it comes to soil and nutrients. They can stay in cell trays until they reach 4 to 5 cm (1.5" to 2.5") and are big enough to be transplanted into a sunny herb garden. These plants are not hardy all over the country, so some may need to be sown anew each year.

## Common garden pots

You can seed start vegetables in common garden pots. Many of the sturdier plants are not good candidates to be started in cell trays—plants such as melon, cucumber, pumpkin, squash, chili and bell peppers, cape gooseberry, artichoke, and chard (also called artichoke thistle) need larger pots and long pre-cultivation care. All plants of the genus cucumis (cucumbers) can be directly sown into large pots, while others can be sown and harvested the same way as different kinds of flower plants.

## A profusion of summer flowers

For an abundance of summer flowers with which to make bouquets, cell trays work beautifully. Plants such as China aster, marigold, painted daisy, snapdragon and rose mallow are a great fit for seed starting in cell trays. In this way you can start up lots of flowers while only using a minimal amount of space. Transplant them into the vegetable patch once they're big enough to be moved—they should have reached between 3 and 5 cm (1.5" to 2.5") in height—as they're sown and grown the same way as vegetables.

*Left: Cell trays can accommodate many plants in a small area. Still, the greenhouse will fill up.*

*Right: Many plants can be started in cell trays. From the top: celery, snapdragon and cress.*

# EARLY HARVESTS IN THE GREENHOUSE

9

Even when nights are chilly, the air and soil warm up quicker in the greenhouse than outside; by taking advantage of this warmth, you can easily harvest young spring vegetables several weeks early. Not in large quantities, but still—what a treat!

In order to do this, you'll have to start the seeds in store-bought planting or sowing soil, at room temperature, and leave the plants inside to germinate. Afterwards, place the seedlings out in the greenhouse's warm soil in early spring, and if you're lucky the spring weather will bring forth uncommonly good produce.

## Spring's first tender vegetables

The plants most suited to early sowing and harvesting are also the most common ones, which makes their seeds inexpensive. Loose-leaf lettuce, arugula, spinach, sorrel and radishes are all delicate first spring vegetables. A salad made from grocery-store iceberg lettuce, with added freshly snipped greens from the greenhouse, is a perennial spring delicacy. Scallions can also be sown early; their leaves impart a mild taste of onion no matter how tender they are.

Lettuce can be picked carefully, leaf by leaf, and then the plants are left alone to mature. Soon enough there will be plenty of leaves to harvest—depending on the weather, naturally. If it's sunny and warm everything will grow like the proverbial weed; if it's chilly, things will grind to a halt. When the time comes to plant tomatoes and cucumber where the lettuce grew, we can plant new lettuce seeds outside. Another option is to plant new lettuce in between the larger plants, but make sure that the area is clean and free of debris, and keep an eye out for, and remove, slugs.

## Sowing seeds

Sowing seeds in anticipation of an early harvest is done the usual way—in a pot or a flat. Lettuce, spinach, onions and radishes are good cold-weather crops and only need between 5°C to 7°C (44°F to 45°F) to germinate. They can grow faster in slightly higher temperatures, but at that point the room might be too warm. Afterwards, the plants are potted up

*We have already been harvesting lettuce for a full month when the trees start to leaf out.*

*Dill for an early harvest is best grown in the greenhouse.*

into small pots in the greenhouse, and then later transplanted into beds or bigger pots. The ideal condition is when the nights are frost free or around 0°C (32°F) when starting cultivation.

Another way is to sow the seeds in larger, shallow flats with sides about 10 cm (4") high. Fill the flat with soil and pat it down; tamp it down a little more in the corners. Fill it with soil up to within 1 cm (about 1/4") of the rim. Water the flat or pots with lukewarm water from a watering can with a spray nozzle. Then sow in planting soil, leaving plenty of space between the seeds, and cover the flat or pots, following the instructions on the seed packet. Let the seeds germinate and leave the seedlings to grow in the flat/pots. When the seedlings have reached a few centimeters (an inch or so) in height, water them with liquid fertilizer. This way the whole cultivation is done in the flat, and in the fall simply empty the soil and plant leftovers into the compost pile. You can also sow the seeds in cell trays and then plant out the seedlings in the garden bed.

*Early sowing and planting in the greenhouse brings on an early harvest of easily grown vegetables, such as radishes.*

## A little extra

There are more plants that can be grown in the greenhouse that produce earlier harvests—keeping in mind that 'early harvest' doesn't mean the same thing all over the country. In the north of Sweden you can grow pole beans and peas in the greenhouse for early harvest; they grow quickly and easily around twine that's attached to the ceiling. Sow the seeds one by one in slightly larger pots and then plant them in the ground bed when the soil has warmed up. Fresh dill to sprinkle onto new potatoes, basil, and other herbs are both delicious and convenient to have on hand, and are easy to grow.

## Pre-sprouting potatoes

The advantage of a greenhouse is that it's a relatively warm and light environment, which in turn makes it a perfect place to pre-sprout potatoes.

The best way to do this is to place the potatoes directly on the soil—a bag of planting soil works well. Place the potatoes on a 5 to 10 cm (2" to 4") layer of damp soil and move them into the light, preferably where it's a bit cooler, to start them sprouting. When the time comes to plant the potatoes, they will have become sturdy plants complete with roots and fine chubby green shoots. They'll grow and yield a harvest long before non-sprouted potatoes.

Pre-sprouting potatoes are especially important now that the risk of late blight has increased. It attacks the foliage, which dies down; the grease-like fungus travels down the stem to the potatoes, and becomes potato blight, making the potatoes inedible. Therefore it's critical that the potatoes get their start quickly, which they will do if they're pre-sprouted.

*Potatoes undergoing pre-sprouting. They will be planted in a bucket in the greenhouse for an extra early harvest. Pre-sprouted potatoes grown outside will also bring on a much earlier and disease-free harvest.*

## Potatoes grown in buckets

Potatoes can be grown in one or two buckets. By pre-sprouting the potatoes and then planting them in buckets, you can bring on an extra early harvest. Buy the early and quick type of certified seed potatoes, and grow them according to the instructions below.

Place the pre-sprouted potatoes in a bucket that has a 10 cm (4") bottom-layer of soil. Don't fill the bucket completely at first - simply cover the potatoes with soil. Water, then water again once the soil has dried up. Place the bucket in the greenhouse. As the potato tops grow, add more soil to the bucket until it's full. The potatoes will be ready to harvest when the potato plant flowers—just tip out the contents of the bucket for a saucepan full of potatoes that need very little cleaning.

# HOTBEDS AND COLD FRAMES

**10**

"In the season when cold is the lone ruler of all growing things, we can by simple means produce the finest vegetable harvests." This is how vividly a leaflet from the beginning of the 1920s describes hotbeds and cold frames.

Hotbeds and cold frames are not common sights these days, and that's a shame because they're a convenient substitute for a greenhouse when space is limited, like in a small yard or allotment. The cost of raw materials is minimal and it makes for a relatively simple DIY project.

## Hot beds or cold frames

A frame or a bed is a simple box, often made out of wood, with 30 to 60 cm (12" to 24") high sloping sides. There is no bottom to the box, so it rests directly on the ground. The lid is a window made of glass or plastic. The volume inside the box is small so it doesn't require much energy to heat. Traditionally, frames/beds can be either hot or cold.

A hotbed is simply a heated growing box. Early on it was heated by composting horse manure and straw together. Composting produces heat and also carbon dioxide, which plants need to grow. Today, hotbeds are heated with electrical coils similar to those used for heated flooring tiles.

*It's easy to both sow and plant in a hotbed or cold frame for an early harvest.*

A cold frame is an unheated growing box. The heat is generated by the sun shining through the glass, which is a much quicker way to warm the box and its contents than to heat up the soil outside the cold frame.

## The old-fashioned method

The traditional cold frame/hotbed is built in the fall and stored away before the cold or frost sets in. A user-friendly box for today's garden is a simple 'raised bed' version of a cold frame. Even though it's a simple construction, it's still very handy in helping to grow early vegetables when you run out of space in the greenhouse. Besides, it's easier to cultivate vegetables in the raised cold frame compared to a conventional garden patch, as there's little need to bend all the way to the ground. In fact, raised-beds have made gardening much more accessible to people with limited mobility and those who use wheelchairs.

The simplest way to set up your own cold frame is to buy or build a wooden raised bed border, and cover it with a plain sheet of fluted plastic to use as a window lid.

## How to's—Cultivating in a hotbed/cold frame

◆ In the fall, place the raised bed border in its assigned spot. Fill it completely with dry leaves or similar material, and cover it with the plastic sheet window/lid. The leaves will insulate the ground against the cold and prevent the frost from penetrating into it too deeply. Carpets made of mineral wool, fiberglass, or other insulating material can also be used.

◆ You can start cultivating in the frame once the spring light starts to shine. Buy bagged planting soil and leave it inside for a few days to warm up a little. Remove the insulating material from the frame and fill it with soil up to within 10 cm (4") of the rim. Cover it with the window lid. (You can attach a soil thermometer to better gauge the warmth of the bed.)

◆ After a few days you'll be able to sow cold-hardy plants such as lettuce, radishes and spinach. Alternatively, you can put those same plants, started from seed, directly outside.

*Not only is the time shorter between sowing and harvesting in a raised bed, it's also easier to sow and plant in one.*

◆ Cover the box with the window at night, and remove the cover from the box in the morning, so that the warmth from the day's sun can be absorbed by the soil; that way the soil doesn't cool down as much at night. In the past, the windows were covered with straw mats that were kept rolled up during the day. Today you can use rugs, woven blinds, several layers of thick cloth, old blankets, or specially plasticized insulating mats as cover. The important thing is that they dry out completely after a rainfall and don't stay waterlogged.

◆ Air out the box on sunny days. The small amount of air trapped between soil and glass or plastic cover can heat up quickly, and while we want to use this warmth we can't let the inside of the box get too hot. To air it out, simply prop open the window with wooden wedges between the window and frame rim. The size of the opening will depend on how far in the wedges are pushed and which side is used.

## The old-fashioned way

Traditionally, as the sun made its way across the sky during the day, the window of the frame was opened and closed at different degrees according to the time of day—a little bit at daybreak, then gradually some more, perhaps even to the point of removing the whole window at midday. Later the top was reattached but still kept open, and then closed for the night around 3 or 4 pm. This is an impractical routine to keep up with today, as it would require you to be in the vicinity of the cold frame at all times. Still, some monitoring needs to take place in the morning and at night, so you might want to use frame windows made of fluted plastic that have automatic openers that look a little like window vents on a greenhouse roof.

A classically built cold frame is 180 x 360 cm (5.9 x 11.8 feet) for three windows which are 180 x 120 cm (5.9 x 3.95 feet); or 150 x 300 cm (4.9 x 9.84 feet) for two windows measuring 150 x 100 cm (4.9 x 3.28 feet). The frame sides are usually 20 to 22 cm (8 to 8 ½ inches) high, and several frame sides are stacked on top of one another. The last one is higher at the back and lower at the front to make the window lid slope - preferably towards southern exposure so a maximum of light and warmth can enter the box. When first sowing and while the seedlings are still small, only the top enclosures of the box need to be in place—additional sides are subsequently added to the frame to make headroom for the growing plants.

Of course, nowadays the frame size can be adapted to each site, as you're no longer dependent on window size for your cold frame top. Instead, you can use sheets of fluted plastic for your lid, so the top size no longer needs to fit a specific window measurement. Old salvaged windows are also fine to use. In this case it's better to use several small windows rather than a single large one. If they're made of glass they'll be very heavy; if they're plastic they'll be light but might blow off and away in a strong wind. Plastic windows can be attached to the wooden side with a hinge. Pre-fabricated cold frames are usually outfitted with hinges, too.

## Plants for pre-cultivation and growing in hotbeds/cold frames

Celery, *Apium groveolens*
Plants from the cabbage family (i.e., cauliflower and broccoli), *Brassica*
Cantaloupe, *Cucumis melo*
Cornichons, pickles, *Cucumis sativus*
Squash, summer squash, winter squash, *Cucurbita*
Lettuce, *Lactuca*
Ground cherry, Cape gooseberry, Tomatillo, *Physalis*
Potato, *Solanum tuberosum*—requires pre-germination four to six weeks on soil in a well-lit area
Bush tomato, *Solanum lycopersicum*
Spinach, *Spinacia oleracea*

## Plants for direct seeding in cold frame/hotbed, and for early harvest

Onion, from onion sets and seed, *Allium*
Scallion, spring onion, *Allium fistulosum*
Dill, *Anethum groveolens*
Beetroot, *Beta vulgaris*
Carrot, *Daucus carota ssp.sativus*
Arugula, *Eruca*
Lettuce, *Latuca*
Sugar snap pea, *Pisum sativum*
Radish, *Raphanus sativus*
Spinach, *Spinacia aleracea*

Many flowers can be cultivated in frames/beds to make beautiful bouquets. A trellis placed at the back of the frame/bed makes an excellent place for squash, pole beans, sweet peas, scarlet beans and climbing plants to grow.

The cold frame/hotbed complements the greenhouse.

A row tunnel made of fiber cloth provides extra warmth and protection.

## Summer harvest

Later in the spring, the cold frame/hotbed can be used for heat loving plants such as melon, tomato, and cucumber. Attaching an out-turning thin metal rim around the raised bed's edge protects plants against slugs, which are a constant problem. When nights are still cold and the plants are young, cover up the plants during the night. Over the peak of summer, however, leave them uncovered day and night, without the window top on. When fall and the first frost arrive, cover the frame/bed again to prolong the harvesting season. Delicate plants like dill and beans, which are difficult to get to germinate and which need warm and loose soil, are also well suited to be grown in cold frames/hotbeds.

## Frame garden

Planting in boxes, frames or pallet collars is a very simple way to garden. If you replenish them every year with bagged weed-free soil, you'll hardly have to weed at all. It's easy to irrigate the loose soil, so plants thrive. The growing surface is elevated, which makes the plants easier to tend to. Strawberries, for example, are rewarding to grow in a framed garden, as they otherwise require a lot of work. Pre-sprouted potatoes can be planted in the frame and can be harvested early. After they're done, lettuce or some other fast-growing green leafy vegetable can be planted in the same soil. Herb gardens can also be grown in frames.

Several raised beds or frames can be placed side by side, and the ground between them covered with flat pavers. This makes for an easy-to-care for planting area where the warmth absorbed by the paving stones during the daytime lingers through the night. Each spring, renew the beds with new bags of healthy soil, and avoid planting the same plants in the same area two years in a row. This type of raised bed garden makes a great complement to your greenhouse.

## Textile covers and tunnels

Another variation of greenhouse gardening is to use growing tunnels. It's the same idea, that is, the ground is covered to keep in the warmth. As with everything, there are more or less intricate ways of doing this. A simple option is to use hoop-shaped PVC tubing across a narrow, 80 to 120 cm (2.6 to 3.28 feet) in-ground bed. Place several tubing hoops in a row across the bed, set 140 to 180 cm (4.6 to 5.9 feet) apart. Cover them with wide, white or translucent plastic, or white floating fabric cover, to make a long, narrow tent.

Set up the tent a few weeks prior to sowing time to give the soil enough time to warm up, then move the cover aside and weed thoroughly. Level the soil, sow, and irrigate as usual. Return the cover and fasten it securely to the bed. Sand bags, stones, or tent stakes work well for this. Seedlings or plants in cell trays can also be grown in tunnels.

The cover protects the plants against flying pests like the *diamondback moth* and the *carrot fly*. To ensure full protection, the plants need to be covered during most of the summer. The cover can also be fitted across beds/frames. Tube holders are screwed down to the wooden frame itself and then the cover is draped across.

Using small moveable plastic huts to cover certain plants is another idea. An open plastic tent is perfect for bush tomatoes if their growing area is open and windy.

## Early strawberry harvest

Strawberries are perennials. They're planted in frames and covered during the winter and early spring with glass to make them flower early. Remove the glass to allow insects to pollinate the flowers; a floating row cover must then be used during ripening to protect against disease and pests, as well as to speed up the ripening.

In the greenhouse, strawberry plants can either be planted in large pots or in the ground. It's very important to help pollination along early on, because bees won't be out if it's too cold and there won't be any fruit. You can lend a hand with this task by using a small brush, just to be on the safe side.

*The classical way to grow strawberries was in the greenhouse. At Sofiero, the Swedish Royal summer retreat, tradition held that the king be served fresh strawberries on the 1st of May.*

*Early summer greenery in the garden beds. In front are asparagus, behind are seed-started onions and pre-sprouted potatoes that were covered by a floating row cover.*

# A GREENHOUSE IN FLOWER YEAR-ROUND

If your aim is to turn your greenhouse into a lush, fragrant and flowering oasis, you'll need plants. Large, easy-to-care-for pots can be moved around as needed to make room for a table and chairs, the space you'll need depending on how many friends you plan to invite in to your sanctuary.

For the greenhouse to feel cozy in wintertime, you'll have to add both heating and lighting to the room. However, if the greenhouse is only to be used during the warmer seasons, it only needs to be heated in order to keep the non-hardy plants alive.

By making use of a variety of different plants—from hardy climbers to delicate houseplants—you'll be able to create a leafy, pleasing atmosphere in the greenhouse all year round. No plants flower or are at their best every season, so you'll want to grow many different plants and flowers to ensure some color or green throughout the year. Many ornamental plants are perennials but are not hardy, and some are evergreens. Many originate from countries where the sun shines brightly and the summers are warm, and the winters slightly cool. It's really a misnomer to call them houseplants, then, as they wouldn't be able to survive inside our houses in the muted light of winter—they need a brightly lit, heated greenhouse. Citrus, camellia, myrtle, pomegranate, rosemary, bay leaf, olive tree and figs are such plants. They would lend a distinctly Mediterranean air to the greenhouse.

Other perennials—even those able to thrive outside year round in our climate—can supply added splendor to the greenhouse. Climbers have lush foliage yet don't take up a lot of floor space. The grape vine is a traditional climbing plant grown in greenhouses—one of its draws being that it's relatively hardy and can survive winter in an unheated enclosure. It also produces beautiful leaves that provide some well-needed shade on sunny summer days. The flowering clematis is also hardy and can be planted in-ground. There are cultivars that flower in early spring, summer and fall, so if you sow a combination of early and late blooming plants, you'll be able to enjoy a variety of gorgeous

*Citrus, figs and flowering rosemary all provide a Mediterranean feel.*

flowers continuously throughout the growing season. The hardiness of roses can occasionally be a bit unpredictable, but thanks to the shelter of the greenhouse you can rely on seeing many more of those flowers come up (as long as no deer drop in for a visit). Potted roses will also bloom earlier and longer. Bougainvillea and passionflower need warmth and thrive up near the ceiling—they will suffer if kept in the living room's dim winter light—and require plenty of light and a frost-free place to stay in the winter. This applies to the potato vine, too, which is a sturdy, vigorous climber with white flowers. Temperatures cannot dip below 0°C (32°F) when growing such exotic climbers; the air should be kept around 5°C to 10°C (41°F to 50°F), even if these plants can withstand one or two chillier nights. They're ideal companions to citrus plants.

## Spring delights

While each season has its own particular charm, you can force spring flowers into bloom earlier in the greenhouse. Whether they're your own forced bulbs or come from the nursery, they all provide great bursts of color when grown in pots, and last longer in the greenhouse, thanks to its cooler nighttime temperature. Demanding light-seekers, such as primulas and the first early geraniums, also bring delight whether they're from your own cultivation or store bought plants. Many of the summer flowers ready for transplanting outside create as pleasant a room as does the first humble pot of springtime perennials, of which you can find a wide selection to choose from at garden centers. Perennials overwintered in the greenhouse will also flower earlier. Peaches, nectarines and apricots—all showy with pretty pink flowers in the spring—can be grown in large containers in the greenhouse. These plants are hardy and don't need a frost-free room since they go dormant in the winter. On the calendar, alpine clematis is the first of the climbers to flower—displaying lovely blue and pink blooms.

*Plants waiting to be transplanted out enjoy the company of store-bought geraniums.*

*Water helps to cool the greenhouse. Myrtle thrives year round as long as there is no risk of frost.*

## Flowers in the summertime

Many plants do better in a warm greenhouse than outside. The enclosure gives us ample opportunity to try all different kinds of flowers in order to find out which ones we like best. Blue potato bush and lantana both put on a beautiful flower show. Both can be trained up as trees, providing a charming accent to the greenhouse.

Small trees (created by training up) such as hibiscus, cape mallow and other houseplants, can sometimes be found at garden centers. They're well worth trying out, even though there's no guarantee they'll survive the winter.

Heliotrope releases its sweet, heady scent on summer evenings. Many salvias are perennials, although they're not hardy plants; they come in many colors and shapes. Some grow almost to the size of a small tree. Luminous gentian sage and scented red pineapple sage, violet mealycup sage and many more beauties like petunias, marguerite daisy and more

traditional bedding plants offer up a fantastic array of rich colors. Some plants like browallia (sapphire flower), coleus, New Guinea impatiens and garden impatiens can be used both as bedding plants and houseplants (which also benefit largely from staying in the greenhouse during the summer. See more on houseplants, chapter 14, page 129.)

Annual climbing vines provide the lush, welcoming, flower-filled atmosphere we imagine a greenhouse to have. Morning glories in all their bright colors, scented sweet peas, and cup and saucer vines in dense foliage, all grow perfectly in this environment. Start them from seed and leave them to grow. Plant and train them in large pots; the larger the containers, the denser their flowers and foliage will become, and the easier the plants will be to care for. Do not move small plants into pots that are too large at the outset; they need to be potted up into successively bigger pots during their growth during spring.

Scarlet runner beans, sugar snap peas and haricots verts (small French green beans) are more than just pretty

*The garden mum will flower for a long time if kept in the greenhouse.*

*The last rose of summer bravely faces the elements.*

flowers—they're also edible. Their leaves are bountiful, their flowers decorative and some beans even have different colored foliage. They're very easy to care for, and rewarding in all their simplicity. The climbing snapdragon starts out slightly frail, but is wonderful to behold in full bloom—pink, blue, and wine-red graceful beauty against the greenery. Climbing garden nasturtium, canary creeper and gloriosa lilies add joyful and luxuriant blooms in shades of red and yellow.

## Fall splendor

The colors of summer flowers continue to delight us into the fall. They'll bloom until killed off by the first frost—unlike perennials, which simply go dormant. Roses often stubbornly continue to produce blooms—that's why roses are often killed by the outside cold. They don't adapt well to winter

temperatures and continue to grow, so keep them in the greenhouse for extra protection against the elements. Once fall arrives, potted chrysanthemums—mums—and asters can increase your flower power. These plants have lovely blooms and are well suited to use in bunches of cut flowers.

It's questionable whether chrysanthemums are hardy north of Skåne, the southernmost province in Sweden. You can dig up the complete plant and store it alongside dahlia roots from year to year. This is frequently done, even though chrysanthemums do occasionally make it through the winters outside in Skåne.

Late New York asters seldom have time to reach flowering stage in the north of Sweden because of the early onset of the cold. If you place them in the greenhouse, however, you'll get to enjoy them far longer. Even dahlias, when given a space in the greenhouse, will continue to flower long past first frost.

*Early-flowering plants - like peaches - need help with pollination.*

## Taking care of flowering plants

As there will be a variety of plants in your greenhouse, their care will require a few different approaches. The common denominator, however, is that during the dark and cold part of the year, watering should be done sparingly, and fertilization even less. No plants should dry out completely, nor should they be tempted to grow from liberal watering and feeding. You must also carefully tend to the pots to make sure they, and the area around them, are kept clean and tidy. Remove all the dead leaves and other decaying plant material so they don't help grey mold set in. An integral part of every fall's big gardening clean up routine is to shower and tidy up your plants.

## Small trees

Peaches, apricots and nectarines are pretty simple to keep in the greenhouse. They start off as small trees for planting in large pots, and they can survive some cold. Not weeklong temperatures of -20°C (-4°F), mind you, but temperatures slightly below 0°C (32°F) won't cause any havoc. The trees' pink flowers appear very early, which is one of the reasons these plants don't fare well further up in the north of Sweden. The plant itself survives the cold but the flowers are destroyed at around 0°C (32°F), a very common outside temperature at which flowers tend to make their appearance. The greenhouse protects the flowers with its milder ambient temperature, but a new problem emerges due to missing, yet vital, actors in the growth process: insects. In order to remedy this, we need to step in and play the part of the bumblebee, and pollinate the flowers by going with a small watercolor brush from flower to flower to transmit the necessary pollen. You don't need to add another plant, but the pollen must reach the pistil.

Potted plants need additional nutrition by way of regular fertilizing. Fertilize at each watering while the trees are green and in bloom, and stop fertilizing once the harvest is over. Make sure the containers are watered even in winter—the soil should not to be too wet, but it should not turn to dust, either. Bay leaf, rosemary, olive and fig trees are other good candidates for the greenhouse. Even they can withstand a temporary cool down, but nothing drastic or prolonged. Fig trees drop their leaves in winter but the rest of the trees stay green, requiring only light and to be watered sparingly. Check on the plants to make sure the soil doesn't dry out, and irrigate as needed. When the seasons change and it becomes lighter and warmer outside, it'll be time to start adding fertilizer to each watering session.

## Citrus—a demanding plant throughout the year

Citrus plants are a real challenge to grow and maintain. They're certainly lovely to behold and a beautiful addition to the greenhouse, but they need a lot of light in winter, so you'll need to pick their spot with extra care. Temperatures can stay around 5°C to 10°C (41°F to 50°F), but an adequate source of light is of utmost importance. There are many different kinds of citrus trees, and their common characteristic is that they can flower and bear fruit simultaneously. The calamandin (calamansi, or Philippine lime) is considered the easiest citrus to cultivate, but like all citrus it needs to be planted in nutrient-rich soil. Use specially formulated citrus soil, i.e., mildly acidic sandy loam. Make sure to water the plant even in winter—sparingly, but not to the point where the soil dries out. Citrus needs special fertilizer during the brighter, warmer season.

*Peach, nectarine and apricot trees flower very early. If left in the shelter of the greenhouse, their blooms will last a long time.*

*Citrus plants are beautiful in bloom, and produce attractive fruit that remain on the branches for many months.*

Other plants, such as pomegranate and crenate orchid cactus, also thrive in a slight winter chill. They prefer their conditions to be frost-free and with plenty of light, and temperatures between 5°C and 10°C (41°F to 50°F), although they can handle chillier rooms in short spells.

The myrtle is an old-world houseplant that has nearly vanished due to our overheated homes. It prefers temperatures around 5°C to 10°C (41°F to 50°F), and it grows well together with camellia and geraniums. Camellias are a bit special, since they flower so early—before Christmas if they are given extra light, but more typically in February. Their beautiful green glossy leaves show that they're related to the tea bush; they're an adornment year round. There is an exceptionally wide array of cultivars to choose from, and it's a pure delight to see the blooms appear. Camellias prefer acidic soil; they should be watered with calcium-free water (rainwater is excellent) and they should be given rhododendron fertilizer.

A good way to successfully maintain demanding plants is to install permanent diffused lighting in the greenhouse. This will help them to flower earlier and more profusely; they'll grow better and appear more abundant in the winter.

## Flowering roses

Roses are probably not the best plants to keep in the greenhouse, as their many prickles (thorns) create problems. Modern roses, however, bloom with gusto and without peer to any other perennial plant. They can produce flowers almost year round, but in order to do this they need diffused lighting. When a shoot has flowered, it takes between five and six weeks before it blooms again. Potted roses that have been trained to standard can therefore provide a real splash of color for a long time. Roses can endure a cold snap during the winter, but

*Next page: Camellias in many colors and shapes thrive in the greenhouse. They'll cope with temperatures a few degrees below freezing, but only for a few days. They'll need extra heat to survive, and diffused light for an early bloom.*

*Above: Tempting sweet-tasting grapes ripen in late summer.*
*Next page: The grape vine provides needed shade on sunny summer days.*

it's better to keep the temperature around 0°C (32°F). Stay vigilant in early spring: roses have no innate growth control, so if it starts getting warm they'll start turning green. The greenhouse warms up early, but can also suddenly experience a cold snap. If the temperature dips below 0°C (32°F), young rose leaves run the risk of freezing, and if this happens it'll be quite a while before new leaves appear. As soon as the plant shows some green, it's high time to start watering and fertilizing.

## Grapes

A grapevine is a vigorous climber, bringing forth luxurious foliage and delicious fruits. The best grapes for growing in a greenhouse are the 'vitis vinifera' species, a 'true' grape cultivar. But there are also many other types of grapes—common ones being 'précoce de maligre,' which

are small and green, and pinot noir, which are quite hardy. There are also new specialty grapes, such as solaris and nero which you can find in garden centers, and they can be used for wine making or enjoyed as dessert grapes. These types are marketed predominantly for greenhouse cultivation, or for growing outside in warm areas in the southern provinces of Sweden.

Hardier and longer lasting than the common grape are the fox grapes. These are vitis hybrids, and are better able to cope with the cold and are more disease resistant. Their grapes are small but very tasty, and they can be grown quite far up north in Sweden. The labrusca grape could be a contender in the greenhouse for someone who lives in a really cold climate, as the vine can take on temperatures as low as -25°C (-13°F). It's important to plant the vine in acidic soil or it will not grow. Fertilize with rhododendron fertilizer during spring and early summer. The rest of the time, simply treat it like a common grapevine.

The grapevine is fairly hardy and can be planted directly in the ground. It's an energetic grower and can become very large, but can be pruned and kept small like in a French vineyard. If the ultimate goal is to have plenty of tasty grapes, it's best to prune the vine hard; if you're after the lush greenery, however, less pruning will do. The grapevine can overtake the whole greenhouse ceiling and its foliage can cast a dark shadow; however, the leaves open quite late in the season and it's wonderful to see the vine grow a canopy above the coffee table. Plant the grapevine along the short end of the greenhouse—if it's a smaller, 10 m² to 15 m² 107.65 to 161.45 ft sq. greenhouse. It's not a good idea to grow a grapevine in a smaller house if you want to plant other things too, since the vine will take up a lot of space. You can lay slabs very closely; the area of soil for the grapevine needn't measure more than 50 cm x 50 cm (1.64 x 1.64 ft). Dig a hole, 50 cm (1.64 ft) deep and 60 cm x 60 cm (2 x 2 ft) wide. Fill it with good soil, place the vine in it, water it and then add more soil until the plant is level with the ground. Water the vine regularly through the year right after planting. Beyond that, the grapevine should do well on its own as long as the ground soil is not too dry or sandy.

You can line the sides of the hole that you've dug with a root barrier in order to prevent the grapevine from encroaching on the surrounding beds. Alternatively, you can plant the vine in a box or in a planter atop a hard surface, but for this you'll need a very large container.

Another option is to plant the grapevine outside the greenhouse and train the vines in under the base. A root barrier placed between the grapevine's planting spot and the greenhouse will stop the roots from forcing their way into the greenhouse soil. This works especially well if you live in a milder climate and want

to grow other plants in the greenhouse. Grapevine roots spread far—their growth habit is energetic. Nothing is done to the vine's brown main stem, depending on when you plant it, and on what the plant looks like. Green shoots that start to grow will eventually be pinched or pruned off, but not during the first summer.

## Pruning grapevines

Late in the fall, the grapevine will be pruned down to two or three buds on the brown main stem. The shoots that have emerged from these buds are also to be pruned away, leaving only one or two buds. This pruning is repeated in late fall each year, leaving the next bud. The vine's height increases by one bud each year, and the side branches will also increase by a single bud. This ends up giving the vine the look of a brown, knotty Christmas tree, and that's perfectly OK for a vine that's going to grow next to the greenhouse gable.

The vine's green shoots are pruned every summer. When the plant begins to flower, all the shoots that produce one or two buds from the flower cluster are removed. Soon, new shoots grow on the leaf axils and they are pinched off above one bud. This pinching is done several times over the summer. The leaves are thrown on the compost pile. Shoots that don't flower are pinched off leaving one bud, or none at all. If there are a lot of grapes, some of them are removed, too. To develop into bunches of large sweet grapes, they need to hang freely and unobstructed so that the sun's rays can reach them.

There are other ways to train a grapevine. You don't have to prune the main stem—you can train it vertically towards the roof ridge or drape it over the crossbars in the greenhouse. It's tied up there as a sort of main stem, and the side shoots growing along the stem are cut off instead. This might actually be a better idea than to grow the vine alongside the gable, but check carefully first to see that the vine isn't blocking the access to and the opening of window vents. The vine might make it a bit awkward to work around mesh awnings, insulation material or plastic bubble coverings, but there are always ways to deal with that.

*Surround the grapevine roots with a root barrier to prevent them from taking over the cucumber and tomato beds.*

*The grapevine leafs out quite late. Thus, its shadow doesn't impede the greenhouse light when it's most needed—in the springtime.*

# OVERWINTERING PLANTS IN THE GREENHOUSE

A greenhouse provides extra warmth to plants, so it's an ideal environment in which to overwinter those specimens that are not always winter-hardy. Potted plants freeze faster than their counterparts that have been planted in the ground.

Not all plants make it through a Swedish winter; they need protection to survive the cold. There are several ways to do this, and the amount of insulation and shelter plants need depends on the types of plants you're growing, and where you live. The biggest hurdle for most plants isn't the cold itself, but abrupt changes in temperature. Many plants survive just fine in cold weather and snow; it's an early spring thaw that melts away the protective snow cover from the plants, followed by a cold snap or freezing, that kills the plants. They need protection against direct cold, and also against moisture. For insulation to work at its best, it needs to stay dry.

You must also remember that roots are more sensitive to cold than parts of the plant that are typically aboveground. The soil acts like a large storage facility with heat, as it will never be as cold as the air and the wind, even if the soil freezes. Potted roots freeze faster than roots in the ground, so even the potted plants need insulation.

## Protecting your plants against the elements

The main concern in overwintering plants is that in the fall, they must all be moved into the greenhouse. Keep the soil in the pots slightly moist, and prepare insulation according to each plant's level of sensitivity. Once spring arrives, their covers must be removed and the plants put outside to stop them from sprouting leaves and flower buds prematurely. For early flowers, remove the insulation but leave the plant in the greenhouse, and start watering. Keep in mind, however, that there's always an inherent risk in letting plants flower early in the greenhouse: if the temperature dips low overnight, the early growth might freeze, so be prepared to cover the plants with a row cover if the weather forecast predicts frost, or keep a thermo cube frost sensor activated.

The right time to move the plants into the greenhouse in the fall also depends on where you live, but more often than not it will be when leaves start falling and plants go dormant. Chill-sensitive plants, like dahlias, need to be moved inside a little before the first frost. Many woody plants, on the other hand, actually need a touch of frost to help them go dormant, so they should be left outside for a few weeks after the first frost. Perennials should not be fertilized in the fall, as this will entice them into start growing again.

## The advantages of a greenhouse

The greenhouse is a dry place where no rain and snow can seep through. Dry soil doesn't freeze as hard as wet soil, and there's also better shelter from bitterly cold winter winds. You can shield your plants against harsh outside conditions further by insulating your

*Left: A wheelbarrow full of potted plants.*
*Next page: A greenhouse with overwintering plants.*

containers, wrapping up plant stems and branches, and adding extra layers of insulation around the whole plant.

You can also avoid the hazards of repeated dips in temperature by sequestering several plants in a separate, slightly heated, area of the greenhouse.

Individual plants are more or less sensitive to cold, and this needs to be taken into account when you set up your overwintering plan. The hardiest plants can be set close together, which guards them against the cold. You can take it a step further and bury the plant roots in the ground—with or without their pot—and cover the ground with leaves. Thanks to the dry atmosphere of the greenhouse, the leaves offer great insulation against the cold.

Similar measures can be taken by placing potted plants close together in boxes, and packing the boxes with mineral wool, packing peanuts, straw, peat moss, or other types of insulation—which all work well in a dry greenhouse. Covering plants with peat moss outside would be catastrophic: the peat moss absorbs large amounts of water that would then freeze into a thick layer of ice; if the ice were to slowly melt, it could suffocate the plant. Wrap the plants with plastic-covered mineral wool mats or pack them in straw, wrapping the lot in netting to keep the straw in place. Pliable ground cover mats offer good insulation too, and can be shaped into stiff, protective cones around plants. Thin fiber row covers wrapped loosely in many layers also work well, and are excellent for layering over groups of plants in boxes. Dry leaves, fir tree branches, burlap, shading cloths/sails, bark chips, and sawdust are all useful materials for insulation. If the weather turns unusually cold, stash the plants in a box with a sheet of polystyrene at the bottom; the mat will prevent the cold from making its way up from the ground through the bottom of the box to freeze the roots.

Different kinds of small trees are also highly sensitive to cold. Plants made up of a trunk and a crown of bushy foliage, like standard roses, standard black and red currants, and the like, need extra protection around their crown. The grafting area—the point at which the trunk meets crown—is more cold-sensitive than the rest of the plant. Even a hardy standard growing in the ground needs its crown wrapped in burlap, textile cover, shadow cloth, or similar type of blanket.

Which plants you decide to bundle up will depend on your geographical location. In the south of Sweden a fig tree overwinters outside, whereas in the middle of the country it needs to be wrapped up. Rosemary will survive outside in some—but not all—areas of Skåne, the southernmost province of Sweden. Garden thyme tends to die both in the south and north of Sweden. Ultimately, the best way to proceed depends both on your type of plant and your place on the map, so ask your neighbors, members of a gardening club, the employees of your local garden center, or plant nursery for advice. While there are no sure-fire guarantees, and there will always be wild cards like the weather, it's always valuable to glean from other people's experience, and beneficial to share what works and what doesn't with others.

## Greenhouse winter insulation

You can insulate the greenhouse itself to overwinter your plants. You can place a smaller, bubble wrap-like plastic greenhouse (that can be heated) in the larger greenhouse. All non-evergreens can be overwintered, spaced close together for protection against the cold. Evergreens, on the other hand, need more space—they require a proper amount of light year round and thus cannot be crowded.

*There are many ways to protect non-hardy plants from the winter cold. It is of utmost importance that all insulation material stays dry.*

*The low winter sun brightens up the greenhouse.*

The ideal temperature at which to overwinter flora varies according to the plant. Even if it were easily available, most plants—with the exception of orchids and other tropical plants—don't do well in tropical heat and light during the winter season. Most of the non-hardy plants we cultivate prefer cooler winters, albeit not as cold as Swedish winters. This goes to show that warmer isn't always better, and that you'll need to find the point at which most of your plants will survive. Plants that tolerate a variety of conditions give us leeway to choose the overwintering method that's most convenient for our space. Geraniums can be kept in well-lit and cool environments, but also do fine in cool and dark sites. If they're overwintered in the light they will grow and may even flower; if they're kept in the dark they will go dormant, which means the temperature will need to be lowered to nearly 0°C (32°F).

The list on page 115 shows recommended overwintering temperatures for an array of plants.

*Lily of the Nile—African lily*

# Recommended temperatures (however, not guaranteed) for overwintering less hardy plants

| Plant name | Light | Temperature |
| --- | --- | --- |
| Flowering Maple, Abutilon x hybridum | light | cool 8°C to 10°C (47°F to 50°F) |
| Lily of the Nile, African Lilly, Agapanthus | light | cool 8°C to 10°C (47°F to 50°F) |
| Windflower, Anemone coronaria | dark | frost-free |
| Marguerite, Daisy, Argyranthemum | light | cool near 0°C (32°F), but frost-free |
| Tuberous Begonia, Begonia x tuberhybrida | dark | warm 10°C to 15°C (50°F to 15°F) |
| Bougainvillea, Bougainvillea | light | cool 8°C to 10°C (47°F to 50°F) can go slightly cooler |
| Angel's Trumpet Brugmansia | dark/light | 10°C to 15°C (50°F to 59°F) |
| Boxwood, Buxus | light | cool, light frost |
| Camellia, Camellia japonica | light | cool 8°C to 10°C (47°F to 50°F) can survive somewhat colder temps |
| Canna Lily, Canna x generalis | dark | frost-free |
| Citrus, Citrus | light | 8°C to 10°C (47°F to 50°F) - can survive somewhat colder temps |
| Garden Dahlia (roots), Dahlia x pinnata | dark | frost-free |
| Eucalyptus, various, Eucalyptus | light | 8°C to 10°C (47°F to 50°F) can survive somewhat colder temps |
| Common fig, Ficus carica | light | cool to high 20s (F) |
| Freesia, Freesia x hybrida | dark | warm 15°C (59°F) |
| Fuchsia, Fuchsia x hybrida | dark | frost-free |
| Gladiolus, Gladiolus x hortulanus | dark | frost-free |
| Heliotrope, Heliotropium arborescens | light | frost-free |
| Lantana, Lantana camara | light | cool 8°C to 10°C (47°F to 50°F) |
| Bay laurel, Laurus nobilis | light | cool near 0°C (32°F) but frost free |
| Myrtle, Myrtus communis | light | frost-free |
| Oleander, Nerium oleander | light | cool 8°C to 10°C (47°F to 50°F) can survive somewhat colder temps |
| Common olive, Olea europaea | light | cool—can take some cold, but needs to stay frost-free to thrive |
| Passionflower, Passiflora | light | 8°C to 10°C (47°F to 50°F) |
| Zonal geranium, Pelargonium x hortorum | light | cool 8°C to 10°C (47°F to 50°F) or |
| | dark | near 0°C (32°F) |
| Nectarine, Peach, Apricot, various, Prunus | — | can take some (but not far) below freezing temps, and not while flowering |
| Persian buttercup, Ranunculus asiaticus | dark | frost-free |
| Rosemary, Rosmarinus officinalis | light | cool—preferably frost-free |
| Potato vine, Solanum laxum 'Album' | light | frost-free |
| Blue potato bush, Solanum rantonnetii | light | frost-free |

# SPRING FLOWERS, BULBS, AND PERENNIALS

**13**

Even if your greenhouse doesn't have a heating system, you can still take advantage of the sun's warmth to force early blooms, and to overwinter newly sown perennials. That little extra heat nudges the plants into flowering before the flowers in the garden are ready.

There are many more flowering plants you can keep outside in containers than you'd think when looking at the selection in a garden center. There are perennials such as lawn daisy and columbine, bedding plants like pansies, or early spring potted bulbs. You can spread the joy of flowers through spring if you grow them yourself - you'll be able to enjoy a first round of early blooms in containers and flower beds before classic summer flowers are even put outside.

Typical bedding plants aren't frost hardy, so they can't be planted out at any old time in the spring. If you opt for hardy, early varieties, you'll have flowers several weeks early. Don't worry if timing is a bit off, if the spring is long and icy cold and you end up not being able to plant anything—even if the flowers go out late, they will still flower as they normally would; you just won't have them as early as you'd hoped.

## Spring flowers

To ensure that your plants flower early, you'll need to begin the process early. The trick is to get a head start by sowing and planting flowers in containers late in summer of the preceding year; then they should be kept protected and preferably frost-free over winter. The early sun's warmth together with a frost-free environment (thanks to an automatic frost monitor) then forces the plants to start flowering. As they will have been growing in a pretty chilly greenhouse up until then, they'll be hardy and can be placed outside even if the temperature dips below freezing during the night. Generally, a few degrees below freezing will be OK; hardened-off pansies can tolerate temperatures as low as -5°C (23°F). The growing part is easy. If there's any hitch along the way, it would be in finding seeds in late summer and fall, so try to buy the seed in the spring when selection is at its widest.

## Sowing and overwintering

The most common spring flower is the pansy. It will flower in the year following sowing, and then it dies down and can't be overwintered outside. For pansies to flower early in spring, they need to be sown the preceding August. Commercial growers typically sow their plants on the same side of New Year's that they want blooms, since they're after the flowers, but they do have greater means to guide the climate in which to grow their plants. If you don't have the benefit of that type of environment, you'll have to follow the rules of growing flowers according to the part of the country in which you live. There are many early spring flowers that are cultivated this way; they're sown in August-September and then left to grow to maturity. They're overwintered in the greenhouse, or perhaps in a cold frame covered with insulating fabric. When the spring sun heats up the greenhouse, any insulation material must be removed; the plants are then treated as per usual—with watering and fertilizing.

*Opposite page: Lawn daisy.*
*Below: Primrose*

*The pansy is an early flowering biennial plant. It can be grown in the greenhouse to provide early plantings for the outdoors.*

## How to's—Sowing for spring blooms

◆ Sow as usual (see chapter 4, page 29). Put the sown pots and trays in the greenhouse.

It's important to follow sowing and growing instructions printed on the seed packet. Reputable seed vendors might also include a separate instruction sheet containing information about sowing and different plants' requirements.

◆ Pot up the seedlings in individual pots with good soil.

◆ Place the pots outside under a protective roof. When fall and cold arrive, bring the pots inside the greenhouse. The plants still need a little time to grow before winter sets in.

◆ The plants overwinter in the greenhouse in their pots.

◆ Depending on the type of plant you're growing, it might be necessary to provide some extra heat to keep the greenhouse frost-free during the winter.

◆ By collecting all your plants in an insulated growing cabinet, you won't have to heat the whole greenhouse. You can hang plastic bubble wrap over an open shelf, tape the sides down and heat the inside with a small fan placed underneath the shelf. The plants can also be covered and tucked in with loose layers of fiber cloth. The fiber cloth is very lightweight so it won't damage or weigh down the potted plants.

◆ When the days begin to get lighter and warmer in the spring, remove the covers and let the plants continue to develop. The right time to take the covers off will depend largely on how early or late the spring turns out to be. For flowers to bloom earlier than when planted outside, you might have to provide some warmth at nighttime. Air out the space during the daytime, since no plants do well in 40°C (104°F) in the day followed by cold at night.

*Primroses come in many colors and shapes. Border or garden auricula is an old-timer that was once very popular.*

## Select or reject

Pansies are biennials, which means that they only flower during a single spring. They come in a great variety of colors, types and shapes—pink, apricot, brown-violet and bi-colors are but a few examples of pansies that have come on the market in the past few years. In Sweden, however, the seed selection is not very large, due to the fact that not many people grow their pansies from seed. English seed catalogs, by contrast, are chock-full of delicate dainties. Since spring is long and arrives early in the United Kingdom, the English have made it their tradition to plant out some early spring flowers before summer's resplendence. To meet the demand for these early plantings, their seed availability is suitably large.

It's very rewarding to plant miniature pansies. They're close relatives of the heart's easy (wild pansy) and tufted (or horned) pansies, which are occasionally biennial. They're hardier and easier for hobby gardeners to grow successfully. They sprout many small flowers instead of a fewer large ones, which makes them less sensitive to inclement weather. Their seeds need light to germinate, so they cannot be covered with soil; they must be grown in a mini greenhouse.

Lawn daisies can survive a few degrees below freezing. Aside from sowing them in August, you can also dig up small plants that grow outside and put them in pots (this should also be done in August). Commercial growers overwinter lawn daisies in a frost-free environment at 8°C to 10°C (46.4°F to 50°F) but they are hardy to lower temperatures too. For earlier flowers, however, you must provide them with extra heat—around 10°C (50°F) in the daytime and somewhat cooler at night. Even lawn daisies can be purchased in seed form from well-stocked English seed vendors.

Forget-me-nots should preferably be housed in a frost-free environment to make them flower early. They come in many beautiful shades of blue, but also in pink and white. They are exquisite as companion plantings to pansies and early tulips. Together with lawn daisies, they make a

flowering meadow of pink and blue. The forget-me-not seeds need light to germinate.

The primrose is often simply called primula, even in Swedish. It has many types and hybrids, and it's a common houseplant during winter months. You'll find primroses at garden centers in fall and winter, and it is quite cold hardy. If you don't want to grow them yourself, buy the plants and harden them off so they're ready to plant out in early spring along with other spring flowers. They look very good together with miniature pansies. The primrose is also sown in the fall, but it's advisable not to give it heat too soon—if it starts growing and budding too early, the flowers will be wan and pale looking. The light in January is not strong enough, so it's better to wait awhile—unless you have growth lights and heat, in which case they can be started. Like forget-me-nots, primroses need light to germinate, so don't cover them with soil.

The wallflower is a plant that was very commonly cultivated at the beginning of the 1900s. They were used as spring houseplants both indoors and out. Sown in April, they were planted out as soon as they got big enough. Around October, whole big plants were dug up—soil and all—and were transferred to the greenhouse, where they were kept in a cool, frost-free environment until it was time to force them into flower. At this point, the greenhouse was heated up to around 12°C to 15°C (53.6°F to 59°F)—but not too early in the New Year, as the plants needed adequate (stronger) light to produce attractive flowers.

Today there are newer versions of the wallflower that are easier and faster to grow. They can be cultivated like pansies, and they even tolerate a cold spell pretty well. Many types, but not all, have an attractive scent. English seed vendors sell wallflowers in assorted colors, and they come in all shades except blue.

It can be a good thing to grow some 'common' perennials, and to force them into early bloom so they can be used as outside bedding plants. However, in order to do this, you'll have to provide some nighttime heat in the greenhouse so the temperature stays around 5°C to 8°C (23°F to 46.4°F). Why not give it a go? Columbines are another popular example, and there are many new beautiful varieties with upturned flowers.

*Green plants, sown in late summer, overwinter in the greenhouse under an insulating cover. Spring sun and the heat from a fan forces them into bloom in early spring. If you grow your own pansies, you'll have many containers full of spring flowers.*

*The wallflower is an old-fashioned spring flower.*

## Splendor of the bulb

Bulbs are some of the easiest of all plants to grow. Many flower by themselves very early in the spring. The flower and leaves are ready in the bulb, just waiting for a cold spell followed by a little bit of warmth and light in spring. The most difficult part of growing bulbs is to actually provide an adequate cold snap, and the bulbs need an early winter in order to flower early. For them, winter is when the temperature is at 7°C to 8°C (44.6°F to 46.4°F) and lasts for about ten weeks—although the specific time will depend on what kind of plant you're dealing with, and also to a certain degree on what the previous summer was like. Commercial growers can offer us flowering tulips in January because they place their bulbs in cold storage as early as September.

### Small bulbs

Small bulbs such as snowdrops, grape hyacinth, winter aconites and crocus are the simplest plants to force into flower. They don't need very much heat and light to start growing; they grow quickly and will flower even if it's cold. They will flower outside even in the chill of early spring—they're used to the cold and are hardy even at temperatures below freezing. You can also plant them closely together in regular-sized pots to grow many flowers in a small space. As the pot isn't very big, it's easy to insert it into a decorative container or plant it in a pot outside.

### Large bulbs

Daffodils and narcissus are also quite rewarding to force, and you can even make it work with wild (botanical) tulips. Daffodil

## Christmas bulbs

Bulbs that flower in time for Christmas have been specially groomed to do so. The bulb itself is heat-treated in a special way so that it only requires a very short period of cold to reach blooming stage.

Christmas Hyacinths are planted on the 15th of September and then kept cool and dark until around the 25th of November. They are then forced in light and at room temperature so that they flower in time for Christmas.

Paperwhite narcissus (daffodil) can be forced to bloom in five weeks without a cold period, and the same goes for amaryllis if it's specially treated, or if it's a South African variety. If the temperature is kept steady, you can force them in the greenhouse where it's probably a little lighter than in the house.

bulbs are rather large and need deeper soil to be able to stand securely. The result often looks sprawling and stiff so you should plant the bulbs in layers to get more flowers, but the pot still needs to be deep and wide.

Large tulips and hyacinths are much trickier to handle. They must be kept at 15°C to 18°C (59°F to 64.4°F) and preferably in extra light during the forcing period to blossom beautifully. Hyacinths require even warmer temperatures—around 20°C to 22°C (68°F to 71.6°F—to get going, and then they need a steady 15°C (59°F) during the growing period. The forcing time for adequately chilled tulip and hyacinth bulbs is three to four weeks. Commercial growers use light-treatment on tulips to impart color to the flowers and leaves, so if you start forcing the flowers too early when the light is weak, you will end up with a spindly and pallid flower.

## How to's—Planting bulbs

◆ The bulbs are planted in pots in September. They are placed on a 5 to 10 cm (2" to 4") layer of planting soil.

◆ Layer the bulbs in several tiers for many closely spaced flowers.

◆ Cover the bulbs with some soil, or preferably with fine sand. The sand is to cover the bulb.

◆ Water the pot until the sand is thoroughly wet. The bulbs should grow roots in the pot, but not start sending up leaves. You will need to check on the bulbs, and water a few times during the fall; the soil should not dry out or stay too wet.

◆ If you don't have access to cold storage, place the potted bulbs outside when it's cool—preferably around 7°C to 8°C (44.6°F to 46.4°F), but under cover. When it gets colder outside, move the pots into the greenhouse.

◆ When the bulbs are covered for winter, their soil needs to remain slightly moist. The bulbs need some humidity to grow, but they can't stand in wet soil over winter because they'll start rotting.

◆ Dig holes in the ground of the greenhouse and lower the pots into them; cover the pots with leaves or other types of insulation. The soil in the pots should not be allowed to freeze. Mark (with flags, for example) where the pots are placed.

Cover the buried pots with sand instead of soil, as it'll be easier to rinse sand off the pots when they're dug up in time to start forcing the flower.

◆ Sometime in the New Year, move the bulb pots into the warmth. They also need light to prevent them from growing tall and gangly, so they'll fare best in a frost-free greenhouse or an outside room. Water the bulbs with lukewarm water when they're being moved. After this, do not water them until they start budding—too much water gives rise to long lush leaves and stems that are easily broken.

*Plant the bulbs close together for best effect.*

## Growing perennials from seed

Many garden perennials, in addition to trees and bushes, are propagated through seed. Others such as rock cress and phlox can be propagated through digging up the whole plant and dividing it into several smaller plants. Some you can take a cutting from and plant in a pot, like a houseplant. Seed sowing is a good way to grow a lot of plants, as in the case of lavender for edging a border, for example. There is a huge selection of seeds from which to choose. Many new plants, as well as a few out-of-the-ordinary that might not be for sale as plants in Sweden, can often be had as seeds. It's great fun to experiment with them, and it's such an easy way to grow many different types of plants.

Perennials are sown in May and June, and the seedlings are potted up in their individual pots. They are not suitable for direct sowing in the ground or the flower bed because the plants will have trouble developing if they're competing for resources with other plants. They're very easily mistaken for weeds, and so are often weeded out. Seedlings are also a popular snack on the slug menu and can be eaten up. A lot of plants also take a long time to germinate, or need other special considerations.

## How to's—Sowing perennials

◆ Sow perennials in early summer in a flat box or in pots.

◆ When potting up, use individual pots and good planting soil.

◆ Leave the plants outside to grow, preferably under a roof to avoid hard rain that could damage the fragile plants.

◆ In the fall, move the plants to the greenhouse or to a cold frame.

◆ When the cold sets in, insulate the plants with fiber cloth or mats. Perennials are usually hardy to a few degrees below freezing, but are less forgiving of the chill when they are potted.

◆ When springtime light starts to shine, remove the fiber cloth cover and insulating materials from the plants to let them start growing. These are not forced to green up and flower early, like pansies and primroses—they are just given a more sheltered beginning.

◆ These plants can be placed directly outside before they are green, if you're not in a hurry to see them flower, or if the greenhouse is too full. Otherwise, you can leave them inside.

◆ Water the plants regularly with added liquid fertilizer, same as with the outside bedding plants.

◆ When the new plants have grown bigger and have turned green, they can be set outside in a protected area, and then after a few weeks they can be transplanted to their allotted space in the flower bed.

◆ In summertime, the sturdy plants will flower a first time.

*The later you sow in summer, the more critical it is to overwinter the pots in the greenhouse over the cold season. If you sow in May and June, the new plants can overwinter in a protected area under a roof or in a plastic tunnel. In early spring, the plants are moved outside if they are not to be forced into early flowering. At right: delphiniums/larkspurs are magnificent perennials that are easy to grow from seed.*

## First year flowering perennials

Many new perennials are bred to flower as soon as their first summer, if sown early enough. They will need to be sown in January and February, and pre-cultivated the same way as summer flowers (see chapter 5, page 40). If you're in no terrible hurry, it's better to sow in early summer and then wait for the first flowers the following year—the plants will be sturdier and the flowers more abundant. On the other hand, perennials that flower in their first year not only often flower later than their true time, but their growth is paltry and their flowers not much to look at.

## Bushes and trees

Many trees and bushes are propagated through seed. Many are familiar with, for example, the horse chestnut, with its large brown seeds that are very easily sown. The common trait of many tree and bush seeds is that they take a significant amount of time to germinate—one to two years not being unusual. Some specimens, such as bush peonies and species roses, also need a cold spell in order to be able to germinate. Sown pots will stand in the greenhouse during the winter, where they're protected from excess moisture, as well as hungry rodents and other animals. During summer, they stay outside and are covered by protective netting. Certain kinds of trees and bushes are propagated through cuttings, just like geraniums. These cuttings are usually taken in the summer (it will, however, depend on what type of plant it is) and they're protected against dehydration in a mini greenhouse set within the greenhouse. More detailed and specialized literature is available to anyone further interested in propagation of plants.

## Delicious herbs

Many herbs are perennials that can be sown like perennials, and then planted out the following year. You can oftentimes even plant them out the same year. The most important requirement for many of them is that the planting area be sunny and that the soil drain well—it needs to be loose and sandy, and to dry quickly, or else small plants risk rotting if they're left standing in wet soil as winter sets in.

The most common herbs are propagated through seed. The striking red-leaved, variegated and white-speckled types of sage, mint and oregano often need to propagate through division, which is also the case with many kinds of thyme. The specimens listed below can all be grown from seed. They will grow a 'true' harvest and will produce fragrant and aromatic leaves. One exception is the type of tarragon used in cooking, which is French tarragon—it isn't possible to sow it. The tarragon seed that you'll find for sale is probably Russian tarragon, which is not nearly as delicate as its French counterpart; however, it usually only says 'tarragon' on the seed packet.

**Perennials to grow from seed**

Anise hyssop, *Agastache foeniculum*
Common hollyhock, *Alcea rosea* (biennial)
Columbine, *Aquilegia*
Greater masterwort, *Astrantia major*
Aubretia, *Aubrieta x cultorum*
Showy calamint, *Calamintha grandiflora*
Carpathian harebell—tussock bell flower, *Campanula carpatica*
Canterbury bells, *Campanula medium* (biennial, perennial)
Peach-leaved bellflower, *Campanula persicifolia*
Field larkspur, *Delphinium*
Sweet William, *Dianthus barbatus* (biennial, new annual plants now exist)
Maiden pink, *Dianthus deltoides*
Pinks, *Dianthus plumarius*
Purple foxglove, *Digitalis purpurea*
Purple coneflower, *Echinacea purpurea*
Blanket flower, *Gaillardia x grandiflora*
Avens, *Geum*
Sweet pea, *Lathyrus latifolius*
English lavender, *Lavandula angustifolia*
Shasta daisy, *Leucanthemum x superbum*
Oxeye daisy or marguerite, *Leucanthemum vulgare*
Garden lupin or large-leaved lupin, *Lupinus polyphyllus*
Russell lupin, *Lupinus x regalis*
Maltese cross—Scarlet lightning, *Lychnis chalcedonica*
Catnip, *Nepeta x faassenii*
Oriental poppy, *Papaver orientale*
Polyanthus primrose, *Primula,* Polyanthus group
English primrose, *Primula vulgaris* (former Primula *aucaulis*)
Self heal—Heal All, *Prunella grandiflora*
Coneflowers, *Rudbeckia*
Woodland Sage, *Salvia nemorosa*
Painted Daisy, *Tanacetum coccineum*
Columbine meadow rue, *Thalictrum aquilegiifolium*
Meadow rue, *Thalictrum delavayi*
Globeflower, *Trollius*
Tufted or horned violets, *Viola,* Cornuta group

## Herbs to grow from seed—Perennials

Garlic, *Allium sativum* (often planted as cloves)
Chives, *Allium schoenaprasum*
Garlic chives, chinese chives, *Allium tuberosum* (tastes like garlic)
Southern wormwood, *Artemisia abratanum*
Absinthe wormwood, *Artemisia absinthium*
Hyssop, *Hyssopus officinalis* (can give rose and white flowers but most usually blue)
English lavender, *Lavandula angustifolia*
Lovage, *Levisticum officinale*
Lemon balm, *Melissa officinalis*
Peppermint, *Mentha x piperita*
Sweet cicely, *Myrrhis odorata*
Russian oregano, *Origanum vulgare*
Garden parsley, *Petroselinum crispum* (biennial)
Rosemary, *Rosmarinus officinalis* (not hardy)
Common sage, *Salvia officinalis*
Common thyme, *Thymus vulgare*

## Herbs to grow from seed—Annuals

Dill, *Anethum graveolens*
Garden chervil, *Anthriscus cerefolium*
Meridian fennel—Persian cumin, *Carum carvi* (can be perennial)
Cilantro, *Coriandrum sativum*
Fennel, *Foeniculum vulgare*
Sweet basil, *Ocimum basilicum*
Marjoram, *Origanum majorana* (can be perennial)
Aniseed, *Pimpinella anisum*

*Above: Small lavender plant from seed.*
*Below: Many lavender plants used for edging a 'Bella Rosa' rose.*

# HOUSEPLANTS

## CUTTINGS AND SEEDS

14

Houseplant enthusiasts—with or without interests in any specific flowers—can derive great pleasure from a greenhouse and/or outside room. Many houseplants suffer when they spend winter inside our homes, because we not only get less natural sunlight though the windows during the day, we also tend to keep our heating cranked up too high.

It was easier in the past to store or keep houseplants over winter: They were usually placed in the parlor, a room that was only heated over the holidays and at special occasions. Some homes also featured a glassed in veranda, or had a root cellar or other kinds of cold storage. In order to ensure that a plant survives winter (if there's not enough sunlight), you need to lower the ambient temperature of the room. It follows that darkness in conjunction with higher heat is not a good combination for plants, with the exception of African violets. The best way to keep plants happy during winter is to provide a cool environment with as much light as possible. Since houseplants often require both a lot of light and a lot of heat, overwintering them in a cold greenhouse is not an optimal solution; the greenhouse can be useful, however, in rejuvenating houseplants in the spring. When the time comes to prune the plants and pot them up, a warm greenhouse is the ideal place to work in.

Tall, winter lanky plants that have been pruned and then placed in a cool and lighted area will grow many new and healthy shoots. The change freshens up the houseplants and makes them bushier. Compare the shoots grown during the winter with the new ones from summer—you'll notice that the spacing between the shoots is shorter, the more light the plant receives. On the other hand, shoots with leaves that are few and far between, and leaves with long shafts, indicate insufficient light.

## Propagation of houseplants

Shoots that are pruned off the plants can be used as cuttings for new plants. A mini greenhouse with a bottom-fed heat source is a great tool for growing new roots quickly.

*Opposite page: Amaryllis 'toscane'.*
*Right: Saintpaulia (African violet).*

## How to's—Propagation by cuttings

◆ Cut off the houseplant's long, lanky shoots.
◆ Take the cut-off shoot, and snip off the stem right under the leaf axil. Depending on the type of plant you're cutting, you're left with the top bit and two to three leaves.
◆ Remove the lower leaf.
◆ Fill a pot with soil, tap the soil down, and water it.
◆ Push the stem down about an inch into the soil.
◆ Enclose the planting in a plastic bag, and place the pot in a mini greenhouse or frame.
◆ Air out the mini greenhouse regularly to remove any condensation that has accumulated. Some mini greenhouses feature small vents that can be opened; or just leave a gap between the box and the lid. Turn the plastic bag inside out, shake off the droplets of water, and replace the bag over the planting. If there's a lot of condensation, leave the plastic bag open at the base instead of fastening it underneath the pot to seal it tight.

*A collector's greenhouse filled with all kinds of geraniums.*

A bag or a lid is necessary so the cuttings don't dry out before they've had time to grow roots. Plants breathe out water through their leaves, and absorb new moisture through their roots. Cuttings don't have any roots yet for taking up water, so they must be in a humid environment to avoid drying out. However, there is a limit to how much moisture is beneficial before the cuttings start to rot, so there needs to be a balance between cutting and soil humidity. After one or several days, the condensation will have been aired out, or the excess water wiped off the lid. When the lid shows just a slight mist, the humidity level is just right.

## Leaf cuttings

Rex begonias, cape primrose and African violets can all be propagated through their leaves. One single leaf can produce lots of identical plants. African violets grow new small plants at each leaf shaft stuck into the soil. Other houseplants propagate through roots or rhizomes, such as cupid's bow (also called orchid pansy), or tubers like gloxinia. There are plenty of houseplants from which to choose to try your hand at propagation.

## Seed propagation

A lot of houseplants are propagated through division, like clivia (also called natal lily), or through the formation of small side plants, like spider plants or hen and chicks. Many plants can be grown from seed, such as coleus, parrot leaf, calico plant, and Joseph's coat. The greenhouse is the perfect place for sowing seeds during the warmer season, as is the mini greenhouse (with bottom fed heat) during the spring. The new plants fill out, grow beautifully colored leaves, and flower earlier. Some plants take a long time to germinate, so the greenhouse is their best bet to grow strong enough during this start-up period.

*Many houseplants, such as geraniums and Christmas cacti, like things cool but frost free, with temperatures around 8°C to 10°C (46.4°F to 50°F). At right: pelargonium from seed.*

Persian violets, pelargoniums/geraniums, fuchsias, browallias and passion-flowers are all easily grown, but need a bit of time and a lot of light to grow handsomely. Many plants can be used in different capacities, as houseplants, greenhouse potted plants, and as outside bedding plants. Their roles are fluid, and the greenhouse only increases your choice of plants' function. Sow according to the instructions on the seed packet, and follow the instructions for summer flowers (see chapter 5, page 40).

## Buy cuttings and small plants
There are many cuttings and small plants for sale in the spring, so it's a great opportunity to buy many plants—from the exotic to the more elegant—at affordable prices. Set them in nutrient rich soil and place them in the greenhouse or on a glassed-in balcony or deck, and they will grow and flower profusely. When you move them from greenhouse to an in-house setting they will become deprived of a lot of light, so

*Pelargonium/Geranium 'Carmel'.*

*Fuchsia: 'Rahees Prins'.*

the best time for this move to take place is during the summer or early fall, when there is still plenty of bright light outside. The plants will then have time to grow accustomed to the lessening daylight as fall sets in. It's much worse for them to move them directly from a bright greenhouse to a dimly lit living room, and that's the reason why some store-bought houseplants turn pale and dismal looking only after a week or two.

## The collector's greenhouse

Pelargoniums/geraniums and fuchsias belong to a niche of plants in which there's an enormous range of flowers. For you, the collector, a greenhouse is the perfect environment to cultivate your own specialty plants.

Pelargoniums/geraniums and fuchsias are profusely flower-rich plants, with extraordinarily long blooming periods. Geraniums and pelargoniums are especially suited to growing in the greenhouse because they rarely suffer from insect infestations.

Many rare or exotic geraniums, like the rose geranium, prefer to have a roof over their heads—even in the summer—and are sensitive to wind damage. The stacked blooms rot easily if left in the rain, and the heavy stalks can easily snap.

Plants are usually very sturdy and hardy when they've spent the whole summer outside or in the greenhouse. They'll flower long into the fall, and if they're given an ambient temperature of 7°C to 8°C (44.6°F to 46.4°F) and a glassed-in veranda or balcony, they may continue to flower during the winter.

They can stay in the greenhouse in wintertime if the temperature is kept above freezing. They overwinter better in a light and cool environment, even if they do also make it when it's both dark and cool. While the fuchsia is less sensitive and copes better with both dark and cold conditions, it does attract *white flies* easily, so you'll need to fight them with a horticultural pesticide. Leave the pots' soil slightly moist, and don't let them dry out completely during the winter. There are a few cultivars that can overwinter outside in the southern regions of Sweden.

It's easy to propagate pelargoniums/geraniums and fuchsia in the greenhouse through cuttings—the plants receive light and as they develop, they produce lots of shoots instead of bolting into lankiness. The greenhouse is also eminently convenient for messy work like potting up and pruning.

Another tempting plant for collectors is angel's trumpet. It produces glorious flowers and green, lush foliage. These plants aren't hardy despite their large size and energetic growth—they're best grown in pots or boxes. Start out with a small container, and pot up several times into larger and larger containers through the season. You will soon have flowering angel's trumpet trees in the greenhouse that can even be moved outside on the warmest days. There are many types of angel's trumpet—color and size vary widely—and they can even come in double flowers. Something to keep in mind is that these flowers are heavily scented. They will overwinter well at 5°C to

*Angel's trumpet.*

*Orchid cactus.*

10°C (41°F to 50°F)—the same temperature as citrus and camellias. Luckily, they can successfully overwinter in the dark, so they can be kept in a root cellar, a garage, or a heated outside barn.

## Visiting houseplants

You can get more mileage out of your houseplants in summertime by letting them take a vacation in—and also add a decorative touch to—your greenhouse. Many houseplants enjoy spending their summer in the greenhouse, where they can stockpile needed energy for the winter ahead. They have no issues with overwintering, since they'll be moved back into the house once fall arrives. They benefit from the additional daylight and humidity in the air of the greenhouse, and they're easier to care for because you can water them without any constraints. If you happen to be taking a holiday also, it's easier to ask a neighbor for help with watering the plants, since they'll all be assembled in one convenient location—the greenhouse.

Evergreen plants such as ivy, golden pothos (also called devil's ivy), cissus, rex begonia, monstera and dieffenbachia all need a growing space in part shade to full shade. They can do perfectly well placed on the floor. Flowering plants like hibiscus and wax plant like to be in a sunny spot. However, even they need a bit of shade over the first few days or else they will burn. Cacti and succulents need sun and only need to be watered sparingly.

Take the opportunity to shower your plants often while they're in the greenhouse so they grow healthy and look their best. If you want new sturdy growth, it's good to prune the plants as you're moving them into the greenhouse. Water regularly with fertilized water, but shower the plants with clean, lukewarm water. *Aphids* and *white flies* are common pests, as are *thrips*. The best way to get rid of them is with regular showers and a treatment with a horticultural pesticide (carefully following the instructions on the packaging). Keeping many plants in one location increases the risk of pest attacks—even troublesome slugs can crawl up sides of pots to get at the plants. Collect and kill the slugs, and spread slug bait in the pots if they become a persistent problem.

The greenhouse is a pleasant space in which to spend time, and which allows you many opportunities to develop a green thumb. If your interests pertain to a more specific area, such as orchid cultivation, you'll need—in addition to a significant fount of knowledge—a more sophisticated greenhouse. There are many associations for enthusiasts and collectors to exchange experiences, and to seek out advice and help. In order to be used for orchid cultivation, the greenhouse needs year-round heating, proper lighting and special care—topics that are beyond the scope of this book.

# 15

# GREENHOUSE OPTIONS

## LOCATION, STRUCTURE, AND MATERIALS

Many of us dream of owning a greenhouse, and happily, in many cases it's a wish that's easily granted. If the greenhouse is used to its full potential, the initial cost will be recouped within a few years, even though its true value—the pleasure of growing things—is immeasurable.

The purchase and/or building of a greenhouse need not be complicated at all. If you're looking for a fully functional outside living space or a pool house, however, be aware that those structures are not considered greenhouses, so you'll need to get in touch with contractors who deal specifically with those types of buildings.

The simplest way to acquire a greenhouse is to buy it as a prefabricated (prefab) kit, of which there are many manufacturers with retail outlets in Sweden and in the US. Prefab greenhouses are typically cheaper, without being inferior in quality, than custom designed structures. If there are special requirements regarding height and size, or color preferences, you can often make arrangements with the manufacturer at an additional cost. The advantage of going the prefab route is that important details such as the roof angle, water drainage, and ventilation system, which can be major headaches to deal with, have already been seen to by the manufacturer and are fully functional.

If you're planning on building the greenhouse yourself, you can tackle this project in different ways. First, check out existing prefab structures to see how technical issues have been addressed. A greenhouse built from old windows or similar materials is fine for cultivating plants, but you'll need to keep in mind that the structure needs adequate ventilation as well as sufficient light exposure so that it doesn't get too dark inside—the ratio of glass to frame structure must be balanced.

## Location

First and foremost, you must select a good site in your garden for the greenhouse. There are good areas for this, and then there are some that are less ideal.

◆ A greenhouse needs sun. It should never be in the shadow of outbuildings, hedges or fences, especially during the winter when the sun hangs low in the sky. In summer this may not be a big deal, but a shaded greenhouse will be cool and dark and may turn mossy as a result.
◆ It's best to place the building's short ends to the east and west, and leave one long side facing south. If the greenhouse abuts the wall of a house, a garage, or similar structure, the opposite long side should face south.
◆ The greenhouse needs to be sheltered from the wind. The windier the site, the more heat the greenhouse will lose—and it's important to preserve as much of the sun's heat as possible if the greenhouse doesn't have its own heating system. And if the greenhouse is heated, you'll end up having to turn the thermostat up higher and keep it on longer, thus incurring higher utility costs.
◆ Avoid placing the greenhouse under big trees, since the roots can interfere with the foundation of the structure. Tree roots tend to find ways under the greenhouse and use up the nourishment in the soil. The

*Opposite page: The greenhouse tucks nicely into the garden, and provides both privacy and shelter from the wind.*

*A multi-paneled greenhouse brings to mind a gazebo.*

greenhouse will also get soiled from bird and insect droppings, as well as from leaves and plant debris falling onto the roof.
◆ Opt for a site where the greenhouse can be integrated into the garden and anchored by stone slabs, paths or flower beds leading up to it. It should look as though the greenhouse has always been there, as if it's an integral part of the house and the garden.

## Adapting your ideas to reality

While the above recommendations on choosing a site for your greenhouse may seem easy enough, reality often brings up a set of challenges, making it necessary to adapt these general guidelines to the specific characteristics of your property. If you only have one location available for the greenhouse in the garden, then that's the space you'll have to use. However, being aware of the pros and cons of your particular environment makes it easier to work around them and try to amend the situation. A new hedge a few feet away from the greenhouse can provide protection from the wind; you can remove a tree branch that throws off too much shade. If the greenhouse is under a big tree, roof and gutters will have to be cleared of leaves regularly; if it gets a lot of shade, then the windows will need to be scrubbed free of moss.

## Building permits

In Sweden, according to the public regulations for garden sheds and cabins ('Friggebod'), you do not need a building permit for a greenhouse measuring up to 10 m² (107.64 ft²), as long as you follow all current applicable rules (see page 144). This is the norm for when the structure is situated 4 1/2 m (4,5 yards) in from the lot's borderline. Permits are also easily obtained for slightly larger greenhouses—builds up to 15 m² (161.46 ft²) are currently under review, and might be applied for in 2008. A greenhouse built mostly from glass is not as blocky as a house; it doesn't cast shadows on neighboring properties like a wooden greenhouse might. In several counties you can apply for a building permit over the phone, but that will depend on the location. In environmentally sensitive areas where it might otherwise be difficult to get a permit, it's of utmost importance to select a greenhouse shape and color that don't clash with their surroundings. Blueprints of the project will need to be supplied along with the application, which should not be a hurdle since greenhouse manufacturers keep very detailed plans of their products, including all measurements, outlines and specs.

## Choice of color and design

Once you've chosen a site, next are the options of color, design, and size of your greenhouse. This doesn't really affect the foundation you'll need, since that will depend on the greenhouse's primary use (see page 150).

As you select your greenhouse, you should make sure that it's compatible with your house and surroundings. A Victorian, hothouse-style structure will clash with a midcentury modern house; a modern aluminum greenhouse will be jarring next to the long and narrow lines traditional to southern Swedish Skåne cottages. Both structural and exterior materials make up the greenhouse's overall look.

Most greenhouse models have their own particular advantages and draw-backs. The most common structure is a rectangular house, which can vary in both length and width; small builds are almost square. When a rectangular greenhouse is bisected along the roof ridge it becomes a half-roof house—also referred to as a 'mural' or 'lean-to' in English—which is placed with its glassless side along a house wall, a privacy fence, or a garage.

There are also round multi-frame greenhouses that consist of five to twelve sides—the number of frames increasing in relation to the size of the foundation. There are variations on this style where the greenhouse is built more like an oriel or a bay window, a winter conservatory or a pool house.

In the past, a traditional Swedish greenhouse was rather long, narrow and low, with a steeply pitched roof. At times it was dug down in the ground so deeply that the pitch of the roof started at ground level, which was an efficient way to conserve heat. If you'd prefer your greenhouse to have a traditional look, opt for a design that's long and narrow—it also happens

*A simple homebuilt construction suited to spring and summer cultivation, but not for overwintering.*

*A greenhouse built as an annex to an outbuilding where one of the greenhouse's long sides is the house's wooden wall.*

to be the most efficient building in terms of available space for cultivation. In a round greenhouse, cultivation is done along the sides of the structure and the middle area might be reserved for a seating arrangement.

## An annex to the house

A lean-to structure, with one of its long sides abutted against a house wall, gleans much of its heat from the main house for free. The house wall acts as an insulator; if it's made of brick or stone it will absorb and retain a lot of daytime heat that will then be given off during the night. The greenhouse will also become more energy efficient, as one of its main walls is protected from the wind. From the standpoint of heating and cultivating, placing your greenhouse along a wall of your house is the best way to go. If it also happens to have an entrance from inside your house, being able to use the greenhouse as a lovely spot for your daily cup of coffee in spring and fall is definitely a plus. The main drawback, however, is that the greenhouse might become too warm, so you'll have to make up for that by installing roof vents and vented windows along the roof line. You can purchase prefabricated versions of lean-to's; if you decide to build your

own, you'll have to pay special attention to the angle of the roof—or near-flat or flat roofs seen on many garden room structures rarely manage to provide enough ventilation.

## The structure of the frame

Today's greenhouse framing material is often made of aluminum, which is excellent for this type of structure—it's relatively sturdy and can be spray-painted or left as is. Aluminum will last many years—even unprotected—its color merely a cosmetic consideration. Along the seacoast, with its wet, salty winds, aluminum structures may have a shorter life, although my neighbor's greenhouse, on the Swedish island of Hven, has spent twenty-five years a short 50 meters (160 ft) from the sea and it's still holding up very well. Its aluminum structure's untreated surface is matte and has turned grey over time, but that's the extent of the change.

A wood framed structure is beautiful, but far less common in modern greenhouses. As aluminum is used more frequently, wooden versions have become expensive, even though the raw material itself may be cheaper. A wooden frame also requires a lot more maintenance than aluminum.

*Red follows white, green and black as common greenhouse color. It can be very attractive in the right site.*

Even larch wood, which is touted as tough and virtually maintenance-free, needs some looking after from time to time.

Old greenhouses were mostly built out of wood, which meant scraping a lot of old chipped paint and sanding the wood before applying each new coat of paint. The ratio of structural frame to glass surface was different also from today's measurements—older greenhouse construction used more wood and less glass. In order to maximize exposure to daylight, the wooden structure was painted white to reflect the light from the structure into the greenhouse. This is critical for growing plants during the fall, winter and spring, but is a completely unnecessary step if you are only interested in cultivating in the summer months. The same applies to the ratio of glass surface to frame, as the proportions aren't as important in summertime as during the darker time of the year. Larger greenhouses in the past were also often made of wrought iron—big heavy buildings—and even they were painted white. Steel frames aren't used for greenhouses any more except in arch-shaped Quonset frames covered in plastic sheets.

## Color options

Most aluminum frames can be painted for a fee—and you will need professional help for this because the frame is powder-coated with special paint, and it has to be done before the structure is assembled. The cost of this service can be a tad high compared to the cost of the whole setup, but a fresh coat of color adds a lot of panache to the structure.

When choosing color for your greenhouse, it's important to remember how much of the structure will be on display. On certain models the glass is held in place by wide silicone strips that cover quite a bit of the frame, which means that your preferred color might not end up having the look you were after, whether inside or out of the building. You can also have the aluminum structure painted white to give it a more traditional look.

A wooden frame can be painted white, but stains containing iron oxide, like the classical Swedish Falu red, are easier to maintain than white. Take care to waterproof any wood that'll be in direct contact with the soil to make it last longer.

*A greenhouse built from old windows. An angel's trumpet is in the foreground.*

## Old or new

There are prefabricated wooden greenhouses available on the market for the traditionally inclined, or for someone living in a particularly ecologically sensitive area. If you're thinking of building your own greenhouse, a wooden structure is the easiest to work on, as aluminum and steel require special equipment and building skills.

If you're hankering for a greenhouse with that old-fashioned look, remember that the size of the glass panes is an important consideration. White small-paned greenhouses were commonplace up until the 1950s, at which point larger panes were introduced and became common. In today's greenhouses you'll find either oversized glass panes, or small overlapping panes without any wooden frame or putty. However, if you prefer the greenhouse to have a real old-fashioned feel, use small panes and putty. If you build the greenhouse from old windows, you might need to refinish them first to get rid of the original lead paint.

A special heads up about the Victorian decorative roof finials for sale with some pre-fabricated greenhouses: they are not a Swedish tradition, and neither is the dark-green color that is common to greenhouses in England. To fit in here, the location would have to be rather unique.

## Cultivation station

For someone who's only interested in growing plants and not in decorative details nor in cozy nooks for leisurely coffee breaks, a hoop greenhouse is the best way to go. Steel hoops covered in plastic sheeting are a common sight at commercial growers and nurseries. Their advantage is that this type of greenhouse is moveable and provides a substantial growing area at comparatively little expense. Their main drawbacks are bad insulation and poor ventilation.

## Cover material

An important decision to make involves the cover material for the greenhouse. There are glass panes or rigid plastic sheets made of poly carbon; there's a substantial difference in looks, in how well you can see through them, as well as in insulation capacity and cost. A less common option is plastic sheeting that is stretched or hung over hoops.

## Glass

Glass is the most common and also the cheapest cover material. Glass is clear and translucent; it's an ineffective insulator but lets in the most light. Glass is heavy, so the structure must be able to support its weight. Glass comes in different thicknesses that will influence the potential size of the panes.

Glass panes measuring 3 mm (0.12") in thickness are typically 60 cm (23.6") wide. Naturally, there are more joints in a greenhouse with 3 mm (0.12") glass panes than in one with 4 mm (0.16") panes. If the joints overlap, condensation will build up and moss will start growing between the panes. The advantage of small panes is that they're easy to change out and install. Also, if one pane breaks, it's cheap to replace.

Glass panes that are 4 mm (0.16") typically measure up to 75 cm between the aluminum bars. The panes can be as tall as the side of the greenhouse, or there might be a joint at the midpoint of the window. They're very dramatic and easy to care for, but also very heavy to install and expensive to replace.

A glass roof requires a steep pitch—quite high and pointy—to prevent snow from collecting onto it, since wet snow gets very heavy and could break both the glass panes and the frame. This is very unusual, however, even in extreme winter weather, but it's better to be safe.

Glass can be covered with a thin layer of metal for insulation, although it's an expensive treatment and there are better ways to insulate a glass greenhouse. Tempered glass is good in a public setting because non-tempered glass shatters into large sharp pieces, while the tempered breaks into small, safer square pieces.

*Next page: A wooden structure with small glass panes in French doors. The doors are recycled from a recently demolished house, and have gone through a thorough refinishing.*

**GLASS**
Translucent
Good ventilation
Inferior insulation
Fragile
Inexpensive

**RIGID PLASTIC**
Good insulation
Won't break
Easy to install
Inferior translucence
Inferior ventilation
Pricy

**PLASTIC FILM**
Simple
Moveable
Inferior insulation
Weather sensitive
Ages quickly
Inexpensive

*A homebuilt structure made with polycarbonate plastic sheets and wood.*

*A greenhouse with plastic frame, covered in plastic film.*

## Plastic

There are several different plastic materials that can be used for covering a greenhouse. The most common of them are sheets of rigid double-layer, fluted insulating plastic. These sheets are more expensive than glass per square foot, but they insulate much better. The sheets come in different thicknesses and widths between the flues. Width and thickness impact the insulation efficiency. Even three-layer sheets with extra good insulation properties can be had. Instructions with the greenhouse will state which kind of plastic covering is needed. All thicknesses do not suit all structures, so it is necessary to choose the type specified for the particular structure.

The rigid plastic sheets are made out of polycarbonate and are not see-through—everything looks a bit fuzzy or indistinct. The width of the fluting will influence its appearance; the wider it is the more translucent the plastic sheet will be, although it'll never be as clear as glass and the sheets age with time. One side of the sheet is protected with a UV-inhibitor acrylic layer, but it still doesn't prevent the sheet from wearing out. That

aside, polycarbonate is an excellent material and is definitely recommended for anyone who wishes to cultivate the year round.

Another advantage of polycarbonate sheets is that they're lightweight and thus don't require a sturdy structure like glass does. It's just a matter of fastening the sheets to a wood frame by drilling a hole in the sheet and then installing them with a washer and screw. The sheets must be upright with the edges perpendicular; the edges need to be covered to prevent water and dirt from running down the fluted ribs. Special polycarbonate sheet edge trim can be bought at the same time (and at the same retailer) as the sheets.

Thanks to its being lightweight and a capable insulator, polycarbonate sheeting is also often used for roofs. It can handle more heavy snow than glass can, so the roof's pitch doesn't need to be as steep. Since the sheets insulate better than glass, the snow on the roof might settle instead of melting. Wet snow becomes heavy and can break the greenhouse frame, so it's very important to sweep the snow off the roof on a regular basis.

**FOOD FOR THOUGHT**

Frame

Size

Color

Cover material

Width between posts

Roof pitch

Ridge

Standing height/side height

Ventilation vents

Gutters

Base/foundation

Door

*A greenhouse made of aluminum and glass, with double sliding doors.*

## Plastic film

Simple and inexpensive greenhouses can be built out of greenhouse plastic film, stretched over a frame structure similar to a tent. Often the structure is a steel frame anchored in the soil, and a reinforced, UV-inhibitor treated plastic sheet is stretched over the top.

This is an excellent trial solution, allowing you to do some temporary cultivation. The frame is hardy and can last many years, but in time the plastic cover will turn yellow, become brittle and begin to crack in about five to ten years. The light source diminishes year after year due to the discoloration of the plastic, so even if the greenhouse is not falling apart physically it gets darker and darker inside, which is not good.

There are even plainer versions of this type of greenhouse, where plastic film is simply stretched across PVC tubing. In a greenhouse where light and heat are not a priority, plastic film will do the job just fine— for growing lettuce, dill, or pansies, for example, which don't need heat under the plastic film. So even if your greenhouse is bare bones, plants will still start growing earlier than if they were out there without any protection whatsoever.

## Choosing material

There is no clear-cut answer on how to choose the cover material for a greenhouse, so when selecting the design and the size of your greenhouse, make a point of first establishing its main purpose.

◆ Polycarbonate sheeting is recommended for year round cultivation.

◆ In greenhouses located further up north, polycarbonate can add an extra month to the growing season during spring and fall.

◆ In the south of Sweden, glass often provides enough coverage for the majority of the year.

◆ For an inviting outside room or cozy corner for your coffee break, utilitarian polycarbonate is not as inviting as glass.

◆ Polycarbonate in a wall and on the roof can be combined with panes of glass on the side of a preferred view for the best of both worlds.

*A small greenhouse made of aluminum with low sides and wooden floor, and a simple sliding door.*

Commercial growers often use polycarbonate walls but glass in the roof to maximize the light and to get better ventilation in their greenhouses. Those of us who grow plants simply for the enjoyment of it can compromise by having polycarbonate sheeting on the roof and glass panes on the sides instead. Heat rises to the ceiling, and then most of it seeps out through the roof; you can stop this heat loss with insulating fabric. Glass walls, in turn, can be insulated with detachable bubble wrap in winter. It does hinder visibility somewhat, but it's removed quickly in springtime.

## Size

The size and shape of your greenhouse is contingent upon how you plan to use it. Most recommend that you buy as big a structure as you can afford, because soon enough you may find yourself outgrowing whatever you have. While this is sound advice, there are limits to consider. Building a greenhouse without a permit is limited to structures measuring only up to 10 m² (107.64 ft²), although an increase of the maximum size to 15 m² (161.46 ft²) is under consideration. 107.64 ft² to 161.46 ft² is more than enough if it's only to be used for cultivation. What requires more space are seating arrangements and the workspace itself. If you wish to include a place to relax, you should mock up your seating plan and then measure the space before selecting a greenhouse. Compare it with a room in the house to get a feel for the right size.

More important than the square footage of the greenhouse is its height. Even if the greenhouse is on the small side—only about 5 m² (53.8 ft²), say—it'll still work perfectly well for growing plants as long as the ceiling level is adequate. A small greenhouse will often have short walls, so the only place you can stand upright is at its center, which makes for not only an uncomfortable space but also an overly warm one. If possible, raise the roof ridge so that the head clearance is adjusted, and so that even your small greenhouse is fully functional and enjoyable to use.

So it isn't the dimension of the greenhouse floor area that determines your available cultivation space, it's the total dimensions of its interior. A long, narrow 1.5 m (4.92 ft) wide greenhouse placed alongside a house wall is perfect for growing plants even if it's only 3 m (9.84 ft) long, as long as the ceiling height is adequate. However, if you'd like to include some kind of seating arrangement, you'll have to look into wider greenhouses. If at all possible, select a building where the standing side height is actually 'standing height', i.e., 180 cm (5'9). This is the measurement taken from the level of the soil of the long side, to where the top of the wall meets the ceiling. Smaller greenhouses usually measure only 135 to 155 cm (4.43' to 5.09') high, which can be very uncomfortable. If for some reason you can't manage a taller greenhouse, one way to circumvent the height issue is to dig down and lower the smaller greenhouse into the ground, thus gaining extra height that way.

Heat can become a problem in the greenhouse. A glass house heats up much faster than a regular house, and too much heat is not good for plants—quite the opposite. When temperatures near 30°C (86°F) many plants really take it hard, and when a greenhouse is short and squat, its environment heats up very quickly indeed. However, the more air circulates in the greenhouse, the longer it takes to heat up; to avoid overheating, the greenhouse needs to have tall sides along with proper ventilation. A steep roof also holds more air than a flat roof.

## Door

The door is an important part of the greenhouse, but in small structures the height of the wall is usually so low that the only place to install an opening is on one of the short ends, under the gable. It can be a sliding door or a swinging door (i.e., a regular, hinged door), which can be divided in two sections like a stable door. Its height can vary: in small houses, doors measuring 180 cm (5'9) are common, but ideally they should be 6'5. The width of the door varies also, and here again—as with height—many tend to be too conservative in choosing its size. In a small greenhouse you typically won't need an opening to accommodate a wheelbarrow, but you should at least be able to enter the area carrying a plant tray.

*An older lean-to greenhouse made out of wood.*

Sliding doors sit in frames that are part of the greenhouse structure. If the house is small, the doorframe might protrude outside the gable, which puts you at risk of injuring yourself, and is not especially attractive to boot. Plus, gravel and soil collects in the tracks as you walk in and out of the greenhouse, eventually making it difficult to open and close the door.

A swinging door or a screen door opens and closes like a normal hinged door. It needs to be latched securely to a wall to stay open because it can be a real wind catcher, so while this type of door is easier to install and more attractive, it might be a bit less practical.

The house and door are integral parts of the construction, so your options are limited in your choice of foundation and laying a base for the greenhouse. The base will be under the door and thus becomes a doorstep to negotiate. If you'll be pushing a wagon into the greenhouse you'll need a ramp, which you can buy as an accessory to the greenhouse; however, if the ramp is in place it'll be impossible to close the door.

You can opt to place the door on one of the long sides of the greenhouse if the wall is tall enough. This makes it more convenient to enter and exit the space, and improves the ventilation somewhat; the downside is that it'll encroach on some of the growing area. One solution is to place a door at each narrow end of the building, or one on each long side, as this enhances the airflow yet further, in addition to decongesting the traffic inside the greenhouse. This is an especially efficient way to create more room and ease of movement for those with mobility issues.

## Roof windows/window vents

Ventilation is controlled through roof windows (also called window vents), louver windows, and through the door. There are usually one or two window vents included in a prefabricated greenhouse, and more can be ordered for an additional fee.

You'll want more windows than are included in the kit. A professional grower should be able to open a roof area equivalent to 25% of his ground area, which means that a 10 m² (107.64 ft²) greenhouse should have a 2.5 m² (26.9 ft²) area on the roof that can be opened. If the greenhouse windows measure 75 cm (2.46) wide and long, that gives each window only a 0.6 m² (6.46 ft²) opening; this means a 10 m² (107.64 ft²) greenhouse needs at least four such roof vents.

Roof ventilation is preferable. To ensure adequate ventilation, make sure to purchase and install the extra vents while you're building the greenhouse, because it'll be nothing if not frustrating to install those extra windows once the structure is finished.

*Ventilation window, window/vent opener and shadow fabric. Notice how the joints indicate where the glass panes overlap.*

Add as many window vents as the structure will safely allow. For maximum effect, place them so that every second window vent opens in the opposite direction of its neighbor's. If the house is in a very windy location, place the vents so they open towards shelter.

Greenhouses with sides made entirely of glass are difficult to ventilate through the side. One way to deal with this is to swap out one glass pane for a louver window or a window vent. The advantage to this is that you can create a cross-breeze if the window vent is placed on the narrow wall across from the door—but this is something you need to plan for while the greenhouse is being put together. Louver windows have narrow glass slats that can be angled to different openings; they're difficult to close tightly to shut out the winter cold and thus are not an entirely satisfactory option.

## Window vent opener

Ventilation windows are opened manually by lifting up a catch and fastening it with a peg. A more sophisticated system involves gears and a chain, a bit like on a bicycle; these are wound up and down. The windows are opened in sunshine and closed when it clouds over and turns cold, usually in the morning and at night. This means you have to check on the greenhouse twice a day, and that might not always be practical.

The best ventilation accessories are automatic openers—thermostatic bars. You don't need to install them for all your windows, but you should consider putting at least one on each side of a small greenhouse, and two for each side for a 15 m² (161.46 ft²) sized building.

Automatic window vent openers (thermostatic bars) react to ambient heat—when the temperature in the greenhouse increases, the window vent opens up. These openers often contain an expansion wax that warms up in high temperatures. You can't be absolutely precise when regulating temperature settings—there's usually a few degrees wiggle room—but you can make the opening happen predictably around 20°C (68°F). All things considered, it does a good job of preventing the heat in the greenhouse from reaching 50°C (122°F), which it can easily do on a sunny April day. Heat rises, so when it's 20°C (68°F) up near the ceiling, it's substantially cooler at lower levels in the greenhouse.

Window vent openers are fitted to each window. The wax cylinder responsible for opening and closing the window is removable from the

*An aluminum frame structure with hinged door fitted on the gable end. The house is low to the ground but can be properly ventilated with several roof window vents that face in two directions.*

*Automatic window vent openings are necessary to help cool the greenhouse when temperatures climb. The heat rises quickly in greenhouses, and temperatures higher than 25°C to 28°C (77°F to 82.4°F) are stressful for plants.*

mechanism and kept inside in storage over winter, and then put back into place in the spring.

During the spring and fall, window vents open and close at controlled temperatures. If need be, you can open more windows in the middle of the day if you happen to be at home. In spring you can make the windows open earlier at a lower temperature in order to prevent too wide a swing between daytime and nighttime temperatures.

If the nights are chilly—at a few degrees above freezing, say— daytime temperatures should not be allowed to rise too far. Either you have to open more windows during the day or you must add heat to the greenhouse at night. As the air becomes warmer both at night and during the day, window vents should be left open more frequently. The warmer it is, the longer the window vents should be left open, and at the peak of summer the window vents can stay open both night and day.  Keep in mind that the door is another vent, so leave it open during warm days, and on warm nights, too.

# FOUNDATION

Many hesitate to buy a greenhouse because they worry about the work involved in laying the foundation, which is unfortunate because it need not be a hassle at all. Small greenhouses don't require complicated foundation work. A floor made of stone slabs, however, is a bigger endeavor.

Your greenhouse needs a foundation, and how much work you devote to it will depend on how you intend to use your greenhouse, and if you plan on heating it year round. The size of the greenhouse is not important, as it's quite a simple task to assemble it. For a pre-fabricated greenhouse you would typically buy a base, which is then set down and anchored to the ground of the site you have chosen.

## The simplest option

A very small greenhouse can be placed upon a simple wood frame of landscape timbers, untreated railway ties, or other sturdy timber. The wood is placed on a layer of gravel, on a perfectly tamped down, leveled surface. Dig down 10 to 20 cm (4" to 8") into the ground, fill the space with gravel, pack it down and lay the wood frame on top of the gravel. This foundation model has been perfectly serviceable for several 10 m² (107.64

ft²) greenhouses set in heavy clay soil, in Swedish zone 4, -36°C to -29°C (-30°F to -20°F), for over 20 years.

To make your structure even sturdier, lay your foundation in deeper. The further north you live, the further down you'll need to dig to provide adequate support. Frost, once the soil freezes, can make the ground heave and push the greenhouse askew.

A greenhouse made of glass is heavy, and this in turn makes it quite stable. What can happen if the foundation isn't laid out carefully and level, however, is that the frame can warp and make the glass panes shatter. A greenhouse made out of polycarbonate is much lighter, but it will need solid anchoring to withstand strong winds and inclement weather.

## A greenhouse anchored by concrete piers

Some additional foundation work is required for slightly larger greenhouses, as well as if you want to be absolutely certain that the foundation won't budge due to ground frost. You'll need to dig deeper wells for piers—down to below the frost line, which will vary according to where you live. The well for the pier is first lined with gravel; a cylindrical cardboard mold (called a sonotube) is inserted into the middle of the well; concrete is then poured into the sonotube. Some areas require that you reinforce these anchors with a rebar, which is inserted into the piers. You can buy pre-cast piers that you place onto the gravel layer, to which the greenhouse base—or frame—is then attached with anchoring bolts, or to a wood sill that the greenhouse is then affixed to.

For a small greenhouse you'll only need one pier per corner. A bigger greenhouse with sides longer than 3 m (9'8") will need an additional pier at the midpoint of each long side, too. If the size of the greenhouse exceeds these measurements, then you might need a pier in the middle of the gable, or perhaps placed on each side of the door.

*Piers (sometimes called plinths) with well-balanced wooden supports, where the greenhouse frame will be fastened.*

*A stone-tiled floor requires digging down into the ground of the greenhouse.*

This type of foundation is excellent for a greenhouse that is not going to be heated year-round. It's also a great option for a half-roof 'lean-to' against a wall.

## Foundation for the larger greenhouse

A larger greenhouse with a poured concrete foundation is more complicated to install, since a ditch has to be dug down to below the frost line. Local builders can tell you how deep you'll need to go. Cover the bottom of the ditch with a layer of macadam or gravel, and pour a layer of concrete on top. Onto this Leca blocks (medium weight concrete blocks), concrete blocks, or brick pavers are cemented into place until the foundation is level with the ground. The greenhouse base is then attached to the foundation.

If the greenhouse is to be kept frost-free through winter, you'll need to line the outside floor area with insulation boards, or you can also use insulating cement blocks.

## The ground in the greenhouse

Usually the ground of the greenhouse is a plain dirt surface, except at paths and seating areas. If the whole floor is to be covered and heated during winter, this will need to be taken care of concurrently with the foundation work.

Dig out the ground in the greenhouse to below the frost line. Fill the area with drainage gravel up to about 25 cm (10") below the final,

*Left: Wood sill anchored with bolts. Time to raise the frame.*
*Below: Leveled, flush surface with braces, sill plate, and studs. The blocks are placed onto a layer of sand.*

*The completed greenhouse, featuring budding spring plants. You can provide shade in several ways—with bamboo blinds, for example.*

finished level. The coarse gravel at the bottom will block the capillary capacity and prevent the ground water from rising to the surface.

Put down a 5 to 7 cm (2" to 2 3/4") layer of construction grade sand (for slabs, brick pavers, concrete stone) on top of the drainage gravel. On top of this lay a level, 3 to 5 cm (1" to 2") layer of fine sand, before finally setting down stone or brick pavers, or concrete stone. Calculate each level's thickness so you reach right height when everything in place. The slabs can vary in thickness—thin slabs are fine, and thick slabs can take on the weight of a car. One way to better insulate the greenhouse against the cold rising from the ground is to add rigid foam insulation boards between the layer of drainage gravel

and the layer of construction sand. Adding sub-floor heat-coil mats (like under the tiles in a bathroom, say) is another option. The heating mats are covered with a level of fine grit sand, and the stone slabs are placed on top.

Another way to deal with the foundation is to pour an all-in-one foundation, similar to ones found in houses without a basement, although they don't offer up any real benefits to the greenhouse since you'd then also need to install a floor drain to stop water from pooling in spots. Normally, excess water seeps down in the ground and through the slab joints. However, if a whole continuous slab is poured then the water has nowhere to go.

Professional horticulturalists often choose to pour concrete paths and leave the rest of the ground bare, as this makes it easy to sweep and rinse off the paths and keep them clean. Dirt and moss can make paths very slippery, which can be dangerous, so the debris is rinsed off onto the side of the path and into the open soil. This is a very crafty solution that's worth copying. Using gravel as ground cover is not as good, as it's a challenge to keep clean and the roots of plants will grow through the pots' draining holes and down into the gravel. Pots need to be placed on saucers if they are to be placed on top of gravel or sand.

Wood as ground cover, in the form of grating, is another option, although the main drawback is that it gets very slippery when wet, which is often the case in a greenhouse. Plastic mats can also become slick, and so should be moved inside in wintertime.

Bark mulch and wood chips are not recommended, nor are cocoa mulch and coconut fiber. These materials break down over time, insects and pests make it their home, and it's too difficult to keep clean.

Sand might work, as long as it's kept free of weeds and soil debris, and is replaced with new weed free sand regularly.

## Heated soil

In order to grow plants directly in the ground over winter, the soil needs to be heated. For this you'll need to build simple, permanent growing beds, and include an insulated foundation for the greenhouse according to the preceding description. Inside the greenhouse, the ground soil is left intact. Dig out the soil from the area in which you wish to cultivate, lay down heating coils in a layer of sand, and refill the area with the soil that was dug up. You'll need to place a barrier (a ground cloth made of thick fiber, for instance) between the sand and the growing soil so you'll know where the heating coils are when the time comes to dig up and change out the soil.

Another option is to build a high foundation wall out of cement, and let the greenhouse glass connect to this wall at about sixty to seventy-five cm (2' to 2 1/2') above the ground surface. Raised growing beds can then be built inside the surrounding foundation wall, and a path along the middle of the ground surface makes for a more convenient height to work on the plants. This is a good way to increase air circulation, and it produces a sturdy and cozy greenhouse. As the glass doesn't go all the way down to the ground the space might be a little bit darker than in other greenhouses, but by the same token the risk of panes shattering due to stones or other impact will be lessened.

Walls also help keep the temperature steady within the greenhouse—the heat doesn't plummet at night since the walls

*An in-ground greenhouse built in the old-fashioned style. It works very well, even for keeping plants through winter.*

radiate the heat they've absorbed during the day; likewise, heat doesn't soar in the morning because the walls have had a chance to cool down overnight.

## In-ground greenhouses

A slightly older variation on this theme is to sink the greenhouse into the ground a little, because the ground doesn't get as cold as the open air during winter. Excavate the entire area where you'll place your greenhouse down below the frost line. Line the bottom of the space with macadam, cover it with a slab of poured concrete, or set down some other ground cover such as gravel or stone slabs. Pour footers for stone/brick walls, and build the walls up to ground level. Insulate the outside of the walls with rigid foam insulation boards, or build the walls with insulating concrete blocks. Make an opening for a point of entry by starting all the way down at the in-ground level and add steps up to ground level. Position the greenhouse onto the wall by making the glass start at ground level, but leave the dug-out depth as it is inside the greenhouse.

Cultivate at ground level by removing yet more soil, and replacing it with new dirt, since at 50 to 80 cm (20" to 32") deep the soil is probably of pretty poor quality—hardly suitable for growing anything. Beds can also be built up against the wall—they should be at least 30 to 40 cm (12" to 16") deep, but if this measurement is off by an inch or two it doesn't really matter. The shallower the beds, however, the more careful you need to be with irrigation and fertilizing. If you choose to grow plants in pots or containers, they will have to be placed on the ground.

This type of greenhouse gets pretty warm during the winter because the ground provides snug protection against the elements and stores heat. It's great for overwintering plants, but its utilitarian aspect will never make it a cozy spot for a coffee break or an outside living space you could set up in a more traditional greenhouse. Nevertheless, if you add a heating mat for the plants to stand on and tent the lot with plastic bubble wrap, your plants will be able to survive many degrees below freezing.

While this kind of greenhouse is rare in today's manufacturing, it's still a good option to consider and a very accessible DIY project. With this model, your greenhouse will not be the dominant structure in your garden but it will have an attractive, vintage appeal, and be economical to maintain and heat to boot. If the glass panes are insulated during winter it will retain heat even better. You can also make a complete lean-to of the northern long side, which will then act as heat storage facility. During sunny spring and fall days, the wall absorbs and stores a lot of residual heat, which is then radiated into the greenhouse at night. It becomes a sort of in-ground half-roof or lean-to greenhouse, which is especially suited to the northern Swedish climate.

# 17 HEATING AND IRRIGATION

As a landmass, Sweden is very elongated; its climate shifts dramatically from the north to the south, and it also seems to change over time. The greenhouse can minimize these variations to some degree, but it can't eradicate them entirely.

The old Swedish saying, "If you turn Sweden around, geographically you'll end up in Rome," is worth remembering when choosing a greenhouse. The difference in climate between Malmö, in Skåne, the southernmost province of Sweden, and Rome in Italy, is dramatic; the same holds true for when you compare the climate in Malmö to the climate in Kiruna, in northern Sweden. This means that greenhouses in the south will have radically different requirements from those in northern areas, so it's a good idea to seek advice from locals before you set about shopping or building your structure.

Commercial growers have completely different needs from us hobby gardeners, so it would be unreasonable to compare our wants to their professional-grade requirements. The nursery pro needs to be able to control heat, irrigation, light, and ventilation with a great deal of precision, and they usually raise one type of crop at a time, depending on the season. We hobby growers, on the other hand, often keep an eclectic mix of plants, all with different needs; wishing to have temperatures calibrated to each individual specimen is unreasonable. Commercial growers build greenhouses adapted to the crops they're raising, while we buy house kits chosen according to the size of our yards as well as for looks. The pros have computerized heat and irrigation; we can do little more than hope for a warm spring.

In addition to its surrounding climate, the greenhouse's intended purpose is important. Unfortunately, climate will be the primary influence on your choice of plants. A simple unheated greenhouse can be used almost throughout the year in the south of Sweden, whereas in the north, a realistic timeframe spans only a few months. Further, it's important to distinguish between actively cultivating crops, and overwintering only. To cultivate in wintertime you'll need to warm up the ground with buried heating coils, a heating mat, or hot water pipes. If you only plan to overwinter plants, you'll only need to supply above-ground heating.

## Greenhouses in the south of Sweden

In the south of Sweden, a greenhouse is a simple and effective way to shorten a long winter. Its typically mild climate means that the greenhouse will work very well, without a lot of extra effort, for overwintering delicate plants. With the assistance of an electronic frost monitor and bubble wrap, you can keep the greenhouse frost-free without incurring a lot of added expense, thus making overwintering fuchsia, geraniums, bulbs and rhizomes, angel's trumpet, heliotrope and potato vine entirely feasible. Seed starting of both summer flowers and vegetables, as well as the propagation of houseplants and other plants, will be both rewarding and quite simple to do. You'll have to make sure to ventilate the greenhouse during the day to lower the temperature

*Polycarbonate is recommended for use in the north of Sweden, as it insulates better than glass.*

to stop the plants from developing too quickly, and to protect them from potential cold snaps in the winter. Occasionally, even the south of Sweden goes through a particularly cold period—usually towards the end of January—in which case you'll need to run a fan heater during the cold spell. The snap is usually short enough, though, not to warrant the costly purchase of a permanent heating system.

## Greenhouses in central Sweden

In central Sweden, a greenhouse is a great boon since it allows you to prolong the growing season—spring arrives earlier and fall lasts longer before winter sets in—if you use a fan heater to keep temperatures reliably above freezing. It's also a good idea to have some type of insulating cover to keep out the chill, and a combination shade and thermal fabric is the way to go.

Sadly, it's quite expensive to keep a greenhouse frost-free in that region over the entire duration of winter; you can defray some of the cost by insulating the greenhouse and fastening sheets of greenhouse bubble wrap to the entire structure. It's also good to build mini greenhouses with polycarbonate sheeting and set them inside the main greenhouse, especially for zone busters and collectors. You can lengthen the growing season significantly by building an insulated foundation and use polycarbonate sheets as a cover. While this might not provide enough warmth for winter cultivation, it's perfect for storing and overwintering plants, as well as seed starting in early spring.

## Greenhouses in the north of Sweden

In colder climates, the greenhouse's main role is to prolong the growing season. The short but intense summer, with its long days and lighter nights, causes the plants to develop extremely quickly. The time span from when the plants begin to show green to being in full bloom is shorter than in the southern part of Sweden. Many seeds sown later in the season catch up with those sown earlier, thanks to the bright and prolonged natural light; yet even here, it's still rewarding to start seeds in the greenhouse. During spring and fall you can heat the greenhouse at night, but you should also cover it with straw mats, shade fabric, insulating mats, or woven rugs, and keep the plants inside the greenhouse during the night, tucked in with several layers of white fiber cloth. If you make the sustained effort of covering and uncovering the greenhouse, you'll limit your heating costs while keeping your plants in good shape.

A greenhouse that needs to be kept frost-free over winter is going to be an expensive greenhouse to run, so a lean-to house or one that is partially in-ground is a cost-effective option. If you cover it with polycarbonate you'll save even more energy. A simple greenhouse kit made of glass is very expensive to keep heated year round—even if it's one of the more economical models to buy—because in the north of Sweden you not only need to heat it to be able to cultivate

*A DIY-built cultivation cabinet in polycarbonate is good for propagation and overwintering.*

*At the top: Attaching bubble wrap. Underneath: The insulating drapes are in place.*

through winter, you also need to keep it sufficiently lit. Keeping a greenhouse in cold climates requires far more work and a larger financial outlay than one situated in the southern part of the country.

## Cultivate or overwinter

There is a big difference between overwintering and cultivating plants in a greenhouse during the winter. The ground has to be warm for cultivation to be successful, and plants need enough light for photosynthesis to take place. Without supplemental light the plant will simply wait, rest and hopefully survive, which is not what cultivating is about. To cultivate means to bring about new growth in the form of new leaves, flowers, and shoots.

Most plants need more light than we can provide naturally if they are to grow in wintertime. Our days are darker and shorter than in the Mediterranean region where many of our most beloved houseplants come from and feel most at home in. To get popular plants like lemon, olive and camellia to truly thrive, they need not just

heat but also extra light; they will survive at 8°C to 10°C (46.4°F to 50°F) without extra light, but they will not grow until there is enough light. Their survival is utterly dependent on how much light and heat you give them, and how large an investment you have to make in them is contingent upon where you live, since identical solutions will produce dramatically different results in different areas of the country.

## Winter insulation

An interesting solution for keeping plants adequately protected in winter is to set up a smaller greenhouse within the main greenhouse. These mini-greenhouses come complete with heating elements and light sources that make it possible to cultivate in winter without it costing a small fortune. An alternative is to build insulated grow cabinets to use for either cultivating or overwintering, depending on where you live and what types of plants you're dealing with. A growth cabinet can be fashioned from fluted polycarbonate sheets attached to a wooden frame;

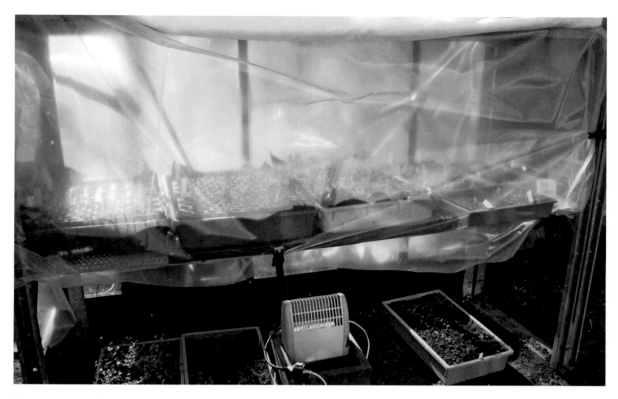

*The young plants have their own tent with added heat.*

rigid hinged sheets act like doors, and the house is customized to hold your particular collection of plants. A simpler construction still is rigid, fluted plastic sheets affixed to a storage shelf; the cabinet can have a light fixture fitted to the underside of the shelf and a fan heater placed at the bottom. An overwintering space can also be made up of tented sheets of bubble wrap and insulation sheets on the ground where the pots are placed; complete the whole setup by installing an electronic frost monitor.

Or pick an area of the greenhouse, then insulate and heat only that demarcated section. Plastic greenhouse bubble wrap (which can be bought by the meter or yard) is attached with special fasteners to the greenhouse frame in the fall, and is left on for the duration of the winter. This material is available at greenhouse manufacturers and retailers (see picture on page 158). It takes less energy to heat a single section of the greenhouse instead of the whole space, and if more protection is needed you can build another tent inside the insulated area of the greenhouse. An inner tent made of insulating material is a good complement to bubble wrap, as it prevents heat loss during the night. There are many different solutions out there; try a few of them until you find one that best fits your budget and/or your plants' needs.

## Insulating drapes

Insulating drapes are used to prevent heat from escaping through the greenhouse roof. They're most commonly used in heated structures, but can also be found in unheated ones. The fabric is set straight across the ceiling—not all the way up to the roof ridge but up to the ceiling joists, then left to hang down the greenhouse walls; special cord attachments help move the panels. The main problem with this method is that it can interfere with the vertical growth pattern of summer plants such as tomatoes and cucumbers, as they cannot make their way up to the ceiling unimpeded.

The very best insulation panels are made from woven plastic with braided aluminum strips (see page 158). Their shiny surface reflects the sun's rays outwards and the greenhouse heat inwards. There's a science to choosing insulating curtains, and commercial growers select their panels very carefully. The material can have different spacing between the aluminum strips, the weave's stitches can be in a range of thicknesses, and colors may vary; you can draw several curtains across in multiple layers for a increased effect. When you buy the curtains from greenhouse manufacturers they'll be able to advise you on the types of panels that best suit your needs.

Using insulating curtains conserves heat; if you intend to install them, make sure to use them diligently during spring, fall, and winter. They can be moved back and forth depending on the weather, which entails a bit more elbow grease but will ultimately save you a lot of money when it comes to energy costs. Before you decide to buy the curtains, however, consider how often you will actually use them; if you incur the expense, you should make full use of them, and not just hang them for show.

It's important to hang the insulating curtains correctly so that there's no gap between the panels when they're drawn. A gap acts almost like a chimney, making a draft that funnels the warm air out of the greenhouse instead of keeping it inside. In the dead of winter the curtains need to be drawn at all times, day and night. If you want to cultivate during this time, you'll have to add light in the greenhouse, which will also give off a little bit of heat. The same curtains work as shade fabric during the summer (see page 162).

*A carpet with heating coils for plant pots to stand on.*

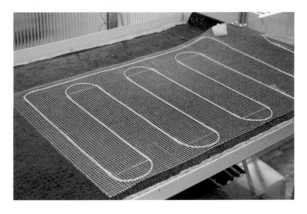

## Heating the soil and the air

If you want to grow plants in the wintertime, it's not enough to insulate the greenhouse with bubble wrap or insulating curtains; you still have to heat the space, and this can be done in a variety of ways. The seeds and the roots in the soil require the most heat, and the seed packet will indicate the temperature needed for the seed to germinate. Ambient air of 20°C (68°F) won't be of any use to a bean if the ground temperature isn't at least 15°C (59°F), which the bean needs in order to germinate. If the soil temperature is only 5°C (41°F) germination will simply not happen. During the growing season the ground soil is naturally warmed in the sun and the air; in winter this source of heat is not enough, which means you'll need to heat the ground in the greenhouse artificially to give the plant the temperature it needs to survive and grow.

### Necessity is the mother of invention

Many greenhouse owners come up with their own ingenious solutions to the challenges of heating their space, just as you will know best what you need and what is available to you. If you have access to free warm water, free firewood, if you can sew curtains or drapes, or if you work as a plumber, a carpenter, or within the packaging industry, you'll have options otherwise unavailable to others and can thus create your own custom solutions. Early on, underground brick piping was used under greenhouses and hotbeds; they created a network through the greenhouses that linked up to a boiler, which was typically located in a workroom in one of the greenhouses' gables. The boiler ran day and night when necessary; during winter nights it was the gardeners' task to keep the fire burning. Hoses that circulate warm water are a modernized incarnation of that type of heating system, and its DIY version is to let all grey water—the waste water from washing dishes, the laundry, and showering—pass through hoses in the greenhouse ground before it ends up in the sewer lines. If your house has a water heating system, you can pull a coil through the greenhouse ground.

Electric coils or heating cables are a flexible, convenient, and fairly common solution for heating the ground (and the air, indirectly). The coils are placed in a layer of sand below the ground bed where the plants are grown, and work much like subfloor heating. They're typically sold already grounded, complete with tripping mechanism and built-in temperature sensor, and need to be installed by a qualified electrician. Special electrical mats for growing tables or in mini-greenhouse boxes also mimic subfloor heating—you just plug them in and the mats heat up. Cover these mats with sand, and secure your potted plants in the sand. If you have a mat in a mini-green hotbed, it'll be both hot and humid balance—the temperature of the ground should be your primary concern. Depending on where your greenhouse is located, you can keep it frost-free and overwinter plants successfully by using only a fan heater. As the plants are not being encouraged to actively grow, the heat from a fan heater is enough to overwinter plants that do not survive frost spells, but will not make whatever's planted in the greenhouse ground start to grow.

There are several ready-made heating solutions available for greenhouses using warm air fans. A fan heater placed on the floor moves the warm air around to heat the inside of the greenhouse. Fan heaters affixed to the walls spread warm air through a perforated plastic hose extended over the entire length of the structure; its advantage is that it's placed higher up than floor level, thus improving the air circulation. The fan can, depending on its type, work as a frost monitor when used in conjunction with a timer or a temperature gauge.

Space heaters are also commonly used, although they are not intended for use in greenhouses; they are unsafe and can even be deadly. It should be highlighted here that all electrical and heating installations must abide by all current and applicable safety rules and regulations.

Less common in use are heaters powered by kerosene or liquid petroleum (LP) gas. There are several similar types of combustion-fired heaters, their advantage being that they give off carbon dioxide that plants need; however, as the heat burns during the night when the plants are not using photosynthesis, this bonus is somewhat minimal. These kinds of heaters also need to be refilled at short and regular intervals.

## Mini hotbeds

Plant propagation requires heat coming up from below, so boxes outfitted with heated mats are ideal for this purpose. When sowing and potting cuttings, germination and rooting take place quicker if there is bottom-fed heat; these same hotbeds can be used for overwintering.

## Temperature

As has been noted earlier, the temperature in the greenhouse is of utmost importance. While you won't be able to control it very precisely in your hobby greenhouse, you can still monitor and measure it. If you use some type of added heating, you should be able to notice its effect on the plants. What is absolutely non-negotiable is a digital maximum-minimum thermometer (see picture on page 182). It indicates the highest and lowest temperatures as well as the current reading. It's best to check it every day during spring and fall, and to recalibrate it so you can keep a close eye on any temperature fluctuations. During the summer months you won't need to reset it or read the thermometer quite as often,

*Fan heater in a greenhouse with brick base.*

in that limited amount of space. You can also place your mats on polystyrene sheets directly on the floor, and place your larger pots on top.

## Fan heating

The warmth of the ground rises up into the surrounding air, which helps make plants bloom. While the gap between the temperature of the ground soil and the air cannot be too great—there has to be a as the temperature and weather are most likely more consistent throughout the day and night.

It can be quite an eye-opener to discover the discrepancy between daytime and nighttime temperatures; the sizeable difference can, in fact, often explain a lot about what's going on with your plants. If you're methodical and take notes, you may find out, for example, why leaves are turning yellow, are wilting, or simply look odd.

If you don't have a heated greenhouse but keep plants in there, you'll need to stay vigilant about monitoring its temperature. If all of a sudden there's a clear night after a bright early spring day, there's an increased risk of frost—especially if there's a full moon—so you'll need to either switch on a fan heater, or cover the plants and the greenhouse with fabric cover and mats. You can also bring plants inside the house for a night or two. If you decide to cover the plants in the evening, it's especially important to uncover them in the morning or else they will overheat.

Elevated temperatures aren't too important for cultivation. Quite the contrary, since many plants don't do well at all when the ambient air reaches 30°C to 35°C (86°F to 95°F); temps around 20°C to 25°C (68°F to 77°F) are far preferable. Ventilate the greenhouse to keep things in check and make sure the air doesn't get too humid, especially in the evenings and at night. High humidity makes it easier for fungal diseases like grey mold to take root among the plants, which is why you shouldn't close all the doors and window vents early in the afternoon in an effort to 'save' the heat for the nighttime, because in so doing you'll only create extra problems.

For that same reason, don't shower your plants in the late afternoon or in the evening; water them only during the midmorning hours. Fungal diseases favor an atmosphere high in humidity paired with cold nights, which is why tomatoes tend to fall prey to grey mold in the fall.

# Shade

One way to lower the temperature in the greenhouse is to stop the sunlight from entering it, either by using some shade fabric, sometimes called a shade sail, or with an insulating curtain (which can also be used during the cold part of the year).

Shade fabric is usually a dark green, sparsely woven net. It is relatively light and flexible, and is a bit similar to burlap. In fact, burlap can also be used as shade material, and is eco-friendly. Shadow fabric is synthetic, it won't rot or mold, and it dries quickly if it gets wet. Burlap is light brown, a bit gummy, and is also quick to dry but is not as durable as shadow fabric.

An insulating curtain is a sparsely woven fabric with added luminous aluminum strips. The advantage of using insulating panels here is that they can do double duty by being used to keep heat in the greenhouse when it gets cold outside.

The curtains can be fastened with clothes pegs to lines, clamped on with special clamps or hung along the greenhouse structure. The fabric is lightweight so it's easy to deal with. If you prefer a more permanent set-up, string the lines along the edge of the ceiling and the roof ridge. Add a channel for a drawstring at the top of the fabric so you can pull the panel across like a normal house curtain.

## Fiber cloth

For shade only, as well as for slight insulation, you can use a white fiber cloth or a row cover. It's thin and lightweight, and can be draped across plants or attached to the greenhouse frame without any complicated pulley systems. The cloth can be sewn, glued, or taped together in many ways; it can also be washed in the washing machine's delicate cycle. Use light lace curtains to add an extra touch of 'pretty'—they make fine shade cloths.

## Chalking

An older way of shutting out the sun was to cover the windows with chalk. A watery mix of special chalk paint was brushed on the outside of the greenhouse panes, the idea being that once it rained the chalk would be washed away and let all the light back into the greenhouse. Warmth and sun in the summer often made for a fairly stable high-pressure system, which could last a few weeks, then 'nature' would take care of the rest. Despite its traditional aspect, however, chalking is not a good idea—it's better to use a translucent curtain—because chalk paint still lets in infrared rays (i.e., the heat), but not the light in the UV-rays.

## Shade fabric panels

Whether you'd like shade in the greenhouse or added comfort to an outside room, you can achieve this easily with shade fabric panels. They look a bit like window curtain panels and span the width of the windows. They are made from thin, stiff netting, similar to mosquito netting, and come in light and dark shades. The panel is hung from an aluminum rail and is moveable—as the sun moves, the panel shifts to cover the seating area. You can make these yourself. Old bamboo blinds that roll up and down can be used in the same fashion (see picture on page 153).

*This shade curtain also offers some winter protection, as it covers the whole ceiling.*

*A shade curtain made of burlap.*

## Irrigation

Plants need light, heat, fertilizer, and water in order to live. Water is used during photosynthesis, and without it no plants will grow. You can't spoil plants by watering them; that they get water every day doesn't mean that they couldn't cope if they had to endure a short drought. Were they to receive too little water, they would still survive, but they wouldn't thrive. Their growth would be stunted or they wouldn't grow at all, with low yields and fewer flowers.

The idea behind having a greenhouse is to provide plants with a spot where they have an optimal chance to thrive; in order to do so, they need plenty of water. It's not enough to water big tomato and cucumber plants once a day at the height of summer. They would probably make it and even yield some fruit, but not to the extent that if they had been given enough water.

It's important to make sure that plants never suffer from a lack of water or fertilizer. When plants wilt, their growth halts.

Automatic irrigation is by far the simplest way to streamline the maintenance of your plants and ensure adequate watering, and there are systems available in a wide range of sophistication. It's a great help even if you only have a few large potted plants to deal with, but for someone who cultivates on a large-scale basis it's most definitely a must-have. For example, cucumbers have somewhat shallow and thin roots but large and lush green foliage. The roots don't have the strength to absorb the water required to keep the leaves satiated on a warm sunny day. If you don't use automatic irrigation and only water the plant in the morning and in the evening, the plant will wilt over several hours in the middle of the day. This, in turn, will make many of the budding cucumbers turn yellow and fall off. Plants abort, i.e., they drop their fruit prematurely, when there isn't enough water and food to grow all of the fruit.

*A drip irrigation hose below pepper plants.*

*Several irrigation drips can be placed where plants need a lot of water.*

### Drip irrigation hoses

There are several ways to provide automatic watering to the plants in the greenhouse, but more often than not it's some type of drip irrigation. The plants receive water either constantly or at regular intervals, during the day and at night. You can use a special hose that seeps water slowly, which is called a soaker hose. A standard-sized foam hose with a built-in pressure reducer is attached to a tap and consistently lets out a small amount of water; the hose is placed alongside the plants growing in the ground. You can't use this kind of irrigation for pots as the hose needs to lie flat, and the only drawback to the soaker hose is that it can be difficult to judge how much water the plants actually get. However, the method is simple and more or less foolproof; it's also well suited to outside flower beds. It saves water and the water goes where it is needed; there's no wasteful spillage, and the plants grow much better when water trickles down slowly to the roots instead of being drenched by a cold shower.

There are also thin plastic hoses with holes that work well at low pressure; the water drips out of small holes or from special seams. Here again it can be difficult to see how much water reaches the plants, but it works well otherwise. These also cannot be used for watering the contents of pots, as they too need to stay on the ground. What you can do, however, is bury them in the ground and the water will reach down to the roots—their intended target.

### Automatic drip irrigation

An automatic drip irrigation system is typically made up of a network of tiny thin hoses attached to slightly larger hoses, which in turn are attached to a main feeder hose. This feeder hose is connected to a faucet, and by opening the faucet to varying degrees, you can control the flow of water that's dispersed.

There are also setups equipped with a small temperature gauge, which is connected between the drip irrigation attachment and the faucet. As temperatures decrease, the rate of dripping water slows down; inversely, when temperatures rise, the amount of water dripping increases.

Water seeps slowly into the ground from the thinnest hoses. They are secured by tubing hold-downs in plastic that are pushed into the ground next to the plants.

One or several drips can be placed at each plant both in pots and directly in the ground. From the main hose you can turn on many drip spots simultaneously; however, the pressure has a tendency to decrease the further the drip point is from the faucet. You can place a measuring cup underneath the drip to check the volume of a drip over a twenty-four-hour period, and can compensate for the low pressure by placing several drips per plant in the affected area.

### Bringing water to the greenhouse

Bringing water to the greenhouse needn't be complicated. A faucet placed by the greenhouse door is convenient, but if water is needed only for summer usage you can simply attach a heavily reinforced

*Drip irrigation is simple and convenient.*

hose from a self-draining water source to the greenhouse, and it can rest on the ground. The hoses can be connected by simple plastic hose connections, although they should be stored inside over winter as they can become brittle in the cold, and split or become leaky. Often all you need to do is replace the washer in the hose connection and it will be tight again, ready to use one more season; washers can be found at most hardware stores.

The situation becomes more challenging if you need year-round irrigation. You'll need the services of a plumber, as the feeder hose needs to be buried in the ground below the frost line and it needs to be properly connected. Hoses for your water supply in summer can be set in quite shallow, and be attached by plastic quick-disconnect adaptors if you don't want them to be visible at all times.

Hoses are available in a wide range of grades. A hose that undergoes constant water pressure needs to be reinforced, because when the hose is exposed to sunshine the water inside heats up and this causes the hose to swell; in the end the hose will burst if it isn't reinforced (alternatively, the plastic adaptors could fail and shoot off like fireworks). A good quality hose is expensive but will last longer; a cheaper hose that twists easily and cuts off the water supply is not a good option.

The greenhouse's thin water transport, drip hoses and attendant accessories for the drip irrigation system are plenty affordable, so buy enough of them to have on hand for future use.

The same drip irrigation system and hoses can be used for pots on the deck or patio if you don't want to bother with repeated watering; simply connect them to reinforced feeding hoses that are attached to a water source. Hanging baskets are a bit more problematic to water, but you can purchase special plastic water—supply containers that hold several quarts of water.

## Automatic timer

Both the hose and the drip irrigation system can be set up on a clock or timer. It works a bit like a kitchen timer, with a special irrigation clock that turns the water on and off at set times, at even intervals, over a span of twenty-four hours. It can even be pre-set for how many times you'd like it to drip each time it is turned on. There are yet more complex systems available on the market, and the more complicated the system, the more expensive it is. That being said, an automatic clock or timer doesn't really offer up any advantages over a simple drip irrigation system that works perfectly well, day and night, without any disruptions. Further, the more complicated the system, the bigger the risk something will go awry; an automatic system takes time to set just right, whether it's to be in use twenty-four hours a day, or be set on a timer.

## Safe vacation solution

It might not feel prudent to leave a drip system on and unattended while going on vacation. Hoses can burst, attachments can fail, or someone might simply stumble over the hose and accidentally disconnect it. Fortunately, there are other options to having the hose connected to a faucet. Drip irrigation can also be connected to a water barrel, where the pressure is controlled by gravity. This is enough water for a few days; you'll eventually need to fill the barrel again. If an attachment fails or something else occurs, the loss of water will be limited to the contents of the barrel, and the leak will probably not happen in the greenhouse. For just a few days' usage there are special kits and drip-watering bags; i.e., plastic bags that can be filled with water and hung on the greenhouse wall, to which a few drip points can be attached. The water won't last long but it will be enough to tide the plants over for a long weekend.

## Automatic fertilizing

Plants need nutrients to grow (see page 26). They can either be added to the soil or to the irrigation water. Hydromat, a Danish product, is a complete irrigation/fertilizing system and a very good investment. In addition to drip hoses, a holder, a feeder hoses, and a pressure valve regulator, the kit comes with a container for fertilizer. The container is mounted high up in the greenhouse and operates through water pressure and siphoning effect. The container is filled with liquid fertilizer, which is meted out along with the water as the water flows through the container, so that the plants are fed continuously. The Hydromat can also be adjusted to control how much water goes to each plant; you'll need to program the amount of water needed to drip over a twenty-four-hour period. You can choose, to a certain extent, the number of drip points that need to be installed. You can irrigate some plants more than others

by putting in extra drip points. If different plants, such as tomatoes and cucumbers, are connected to the drip, it's usually the cucumber that needs the most water, so attach two drips to each cucumber plant and one to each of the tomatoes.

## Keeping an eye on it all

It takes about a week to program all the drip settings for the plants. Start well before going on vacation so everything is working to your satisfaction on the day of your departure. Do a tour of the greenhouse once a day at the beginning and feel the soil; check for pooling water or if there is a proliferation of fungus gnats anywhere. Fungus gnats are small, fast-moving flies that you'll find on humid soil. If a cloud rises up from the plant as you approach it, it's usually a sign of these flies, and is an indication the air in the greenhouse is too damp.

A rough guesstimate is that plants should be given approximately 1/2 liter to 1 1/2 liter (1 to 1 1/2 quarts) liquid a day per twenty-four-hour period, no matter how many drips are generated. Plants that are not given enough water will wilt, but if the soil is very wet and the plant is wilting anyway, the problem is probably due to excess water. The soil surface between the drip points should be dry; plants absorb only what they need, but that doesn't mean that the soil in the pot or in the ground can't be too humid. Roots don't fare well in excess moisture.

Plants will need more humidity at the height of summer than during spring and late fall. You'll need to increase the irrigation when temperatures rise and there is more sunshine; also, big plants require more water than smaller ones. By late summer you'll need to decrease irrigation, or fungus and mold problems might flare up.

*A water source to which a hose can be attached.*

## Showering and misting

A spray nozzle attachment to the garden hose is a common tool in many gardens; while the spray nozzle is not suitable for watering the plants, it is acceptable for showering them if the spray is set to 'mist.' It can also be beneficial on very hot days to shower the ceiling, floor, walls and plants in the greenhouse, as it lowers the temperature and allows the plants to breathe easier. The risk for aphid and spider mite attacks is substantially reduced, as spraying with water is the best way to combat these pests—far better than using chemical insecticides. If the plants are wilting, a shower will also help them to perk up, but the water should be lukewarm, never ice cold.

Misting spray nozzles are mini sprays that attach like pushpins to a hard plastic hose (see picture on page 76).

When the water is turned on, a fine mist is dispersed through the little spray nozzles. Nozzle misting is perfect for cooling down vegetables and improving the pollination of tomatoes. There are ready-made systems available for purchase, and the rigid plastic hose is affixed to the greenhouse ceiling, making the spray come down like a fine fog, which gives the water enough time to warm up before it sprinkles the plants, and doesn't fall like a cold shower. This system can also be connected to a clock or timer, but misting is not done as often as watering. It's enough to manually turn the mist on a few times in the middle of the day as the temperature climbs. Misting is not needed on cold overcast days, and never mist in the afternoon or evening, irrespective of temperature (this is why manual control is preferable to an automatic misting function).

## Extra water and nutrients

Even if you have an automatic irrigation system, complete with fertilizer, it's not always enough, so it's always a good idea to check the greenhouse, watering can in hand, to give needy plants some extra watered-down fertilizer, which might be a plant in a drafty corner or in a excessively sunny spot. Also, check for the signs of malnutrition, which is most obvious in new plant growth. It's perfectly okay for old leaves to turn yellow, but new growth on the top should be green and fresh looking. If it looks tired, try feeding it some nutrients in the form of Blomstra (or equivalent fertilizer) at 1 ml per quart of water for a few days, and check back to see if the plant is perking up.

*A Hydromat system complete with protective polystyrene 'hat,' to avoid the growth of mold in the container.*

The drip feed can dam up so no water comes through. Check the drip frequency by placing a measuring cup under the drip next to the wilting plant. Also, check under the plant to make sure the soil is moist; if the soil is dry, the drip might be clogged up due to mineral deposits or fertilizer. Remove the drip and blow through the hoses to clear them. The fertilizer container might not be working, or the fertilizer might be used up, since it needs to be refilled several times during the growing season. Be extra attentive while checking the irrigation system, not only to secure the harvest but also because plants that are left to dry out are more susceptible to attacks by aphids and other pests.

# INTERIOR AND LIGHTING

The interior of a greenhouse can be set up in a variety of ways, but your primary concern should be to maximize its utility as well as its comfort. A good worktable, shelves, and easy-to-care-for flooring are a must; so are lighting (whether natural or artificial), some kind of seating arrangement, and storage space for your materials.

18

Greenhouses are often wet on the inside, and they're slow to dry; this near-constant humidity makes them the perfect environment for moss and mold to proliferate. If you bear this in mind, you can arrange your space like the inside of a workshop in order to minimize the dampness.

## The floor

A beautiful stone floor will impart a nice homey feel, but if you want it perfectly level with the ground, you'll have to excavate it a little before laying down the slabs (see Ground Covering, page 152).

Elegant brick flooring is expensive, in contrast to grey cement slabs, which can be had for next to nothing. There are many other stone materials to consider, too, so let your imagination and taste be your guide. Large, decorative plant-filled pots look nice on the floor.

You can also level off the soil and place pots directly on the ground, but that quickly gets messy and slippery. If you plan on cultivating in the ground, place stone slabs only to make a pathway between the plants as well as for an optional seating area.

Another simple trick is to remove some earth, lay down a thin layer of sand, and place stone slabs on top of it, although this can end up being a bit unsteady to walk on. The good thing about this option is that it's easy and quick to try, and if the path isn't well set down the first time, it can easily be redone.

## Along the walls

Besides the floor, the interior of the greenhouse is comprised of shelving, worktables or benches, and a cozy seating area; there should also be storage space for bags, pots, flats, and miscellaneous gardening gear. If you're not planning on using the greenhouse during the winter, it can double as a storage area for both plants and garden furniture.

*Previous page: It's a good idea to install shelving that can be dismantled and moved around in the greenhouse. When plants grow tall, simply remove the top shelf.*
*Above: Shelves for growing and training plants.*

Many greenhouses on the market have interior fixtures attached directly to the structure; the shelving and workstation are screwed into the wall in different configurations. This is highly limiting, as you can't, for example, set down heavy pots on an attached table without putting strain on the entire structure of the greenhouse. It's better to use freestanding shelving systems and tables; they're far simpler to move around to suit the weather or to facilitate any task at hand. Plus, no one wants to take a coffee break in the greenhouse at the height of summer; inversely, it may be the coziest spot in the garden if the weather turns cold and wet. Furthermore, you should be able to push shelves together to better store your tools and supplies in preparation for winter. Being flexible in your interior design is the best way to maximize your greenhouse's overall usage and comfort.

Using shelves in the greenhouse is very practical, because it allows you to cultivate vertically and thus have room for many small plants. Even better is shelving that can be dismantled or shelving planks that can be removed, especially since small 50 cm (20") tomato plants can easily reach 5 to 8 m (16' to 26') in height by season's end, growth that your shelves need to be able to accommodate. Springtime will be the most crowded season in the greenhouse if you pre-cultivate plants, as most of your shelf space will be devoted to many layers of boxes with seedlings. You should not place any boxes directly on the ground (even if there are only a few), because it's too cold and drafty at floor level; plants do much better when situated a little higher up—which is another good reason to have shelves or a moveable table in the greenhouse, even if you don't plan on growing that many plants.

The greenhouse will empty out once all the flowers, such as pelargoniums/geraniums, angel's trumpet and other perennial houseplants, as well as the vegetables, are moved outside. At this point you can remove the shelving to get it out of the way and make room for more living space.

Choose frames and shelves made of metal, as the humidity in the greenhouse will damage wood. On the other hand, wooden shelving is cheap; it works fine when finished and is easily maintained or replaced. Applying some colorful paint adds a nice touch and can match your chairs, cushions or planters. Another bonus with freestanding shelves is that they're easy to insulate or shade. They have their own framework, so nothing is attached to the greenhouse. By moving these shelves away from the walls, you can also easily insulate the sides of the greenhouse in the fall to prepare for the cold winter months ahead, which is not as easily done with fixed shelving in the way.

*There is more outdoor living space in the greenhouse once the plants have moved outside for the summer.*

## Worktables

Tables for cultivating, as well as worktables, can be set up on trestles. A rimmed wooden sheet, like an old-fashioned baking board, can serve as a growing table; the dirt stays contained due to the rim. The top is secured to the trestles with the help of adhesive strips attached underneath to prevent the board from sliding off. As the worktable is moveable, it's perfect for relocating outside as the weather allows. When used inside the greenhouse, it can stay in the center of the workspace until the planting is done.

Setting seedlings on growing tables makes it easy to care for them. You can choose the work height that suits you; tables can be dismantled and easily moved out of the way when you want to plant bigger plants in the ground, or place bigger containers on the floor. Growing tables made from removable plastic trays set on trestles make watering easier. They come in various sizes, and their low rim makes it simple to water the pots from below, or to use an irrigation mat. It's also practical in case you want to separate the tables, and have several small trays instead of one large tray.

## Separate spaces

In a pinch, garden tables can be used as planting tables, but typically they're not high enough, not to mention that they quickly become muddy from the spilled dirt. Generally, it's preferable to keep the workstation and the coffee break areas separate.

There are myriad possibilities in seating arrangements within the greenhouse. Remember that its environment is both humid and warm, so garden furniture meant for outdoor living is what you'll want to look for—wicker and rattan, for example, or materials that can be easily rinsed off and cleaned. If you want your plants to thrive, you'll need to be able to wet down the floors and shower the plants on really warm days; by wetting the floors and walls you're lowering the temperature but are also increasing the level of ambient humidity, and your furniture cannot be so delicate that it cannot withstand this type of atmosphere.

*Opposite side: Rimmed trays on freestanding trestles are a convenient setup. They're easy to water, to separate, and move apart. Ceiling light, used in winter.*

*Use what you have on hand. Here's a simple table, easy to take apart, and it can be used in different ways.*

*Greenhouse HPS (High Pressure Sodium) light fittings give the plants much needed light.*

# Lighting

Brightening the greenhouse with artificial light is an option, but not a necessity. If you plan to grow plants year round, or if you'd like to putter in the heated greenhouse over winter, you will need both lighting for the plants and for your workstation. However, if you intend to use the greenhouse mostly for enjoyment and to work in during the warmer seasons, then you won't need any added light source. Besides, what could be more peaceful and serene than a candle-lit coffee evening in the greenhouse?

Lights will be required in the greenhouse in winter if you want to keep on growing plants, not merely to have them survive. Many plants like geraniums will continue to grow and bloom in the wintertime if they have added light and heat. Others, like the olive tree or the bay leaf, overwinter successfully in natural light and a cool climate, but don't need extra light.

## Moveable solutions

The earliest sowings usually take place between the end of January and the onset of February. By February to early March, newly potted up plants will start to need more space. When there's no more room on the light-filled window sills but the greenhouse is still too chilly, then extra lighting might be required in the house, but not for very long (see page 33)—four to five weeks at most, after which natural daytime light should be enough. At this point it might even be time to move your plants into the greenhouse.

If you have to cultivate your plants in a space without windows—in the basement or in the garage, say—you can add permanent lighting in that area. As for the short weeks in spring when your plants require extra light, you can deal with this issue pretty simply and temporarily, even if you only use the greenhouse for a short period of time.

## Lighting in the greenhouse

Proper light fixtures for permanent greenhouse lighting can be both expensive and heavy. In order to light a large area, the lights have to be set high up, and so must also be of strong enough wattage to shine brightly onto the plants. Commercial growers use HPS (High Pressure Sodium) in special fixtures with reflecting shields. They give off an orange glow reminiscent of Swedish interstate lighting. A light fixture with a light source of 400W is plenty for a greenhouse measuring 10 m² (108 sq ft). A special mini version of the light measuring 70W HPS is enough for 3 to 4 m² (32 to 43 sq ft) greenhouse if it's placed at about 50 cm (19 3/4 ") above the plants. HPS lights shed more light per watt than their fluorescent counterparts.

Nevertheless, fluorescent lights are easier to find, and remain a very good option for lighting your space; they do however need to be cold white fluorescent lights in order to be used as growth lights. Warm white fluorescent lights are included when you buy the light fixture, and are commonly used to light standard work environments, but they are not good for growing plants. Cold white lights are not expensive; they're simply not used as often because they don't give us human beings comfortable lighting in the way warm white lights do. There are also specific fluorescent growth lights available, but they're more expensive and are not as efficient as the cold white fluorescent lights. Those growth lights are colored tubes containing special spectra for plants, but the plants end up getting less light due to the coating on the tube, so you may as well avoid them.

Metal halogen lights are another good alternative for lighting your greenhouse. They give off a sharp blue-white light; however, they do need to be used with special light fixtures. Plants thrive in this kind of light, and if you're cultivating in an environment without any natural daylight whatsoever, these are the best lights to use. Cacti and other plants that normally get a large amount of intense light in their natural habitat do best in this type of lighting.

## Choice of lighting

Choose lighting according to your needs first. Light fixtures are available at most shopping centers, but the fluorescent tubes typically must be purchased from an electrical store. Permanent lighting should be bought at a greenhouse dealer's outlet, since the staff understand the structures and their potential problems, and sell fixtures that can handle humid environments. HPS and metal halogen lamps have to

*The garden's coziest room is the greenhouse. Pelargoniums/geraniums, here set on fixed shelving, leave room for a sofa and a table.*

fit into special fixtures outfitted with strong reflectors. Typically it's a fixture that can accommodate either a metal halogen or an HPS lamp. The lamps are pricey, but it's nice to be able to choose between metal halogen and HPS lights without having to swap out the entire fixture. This type of light fixture is primarily of interest to anyone needing to light an area over a significant stretch of winter, perhaps a space with camellias or citrus trees.

Fluorescent tubes work well above sown trays and boxes. You can choose fixtures according to whether the lights are going to be used in the greenhouse or inside the house, but you must only use fixtures fit for damp spaces within the greenhouse. An effective setup is to mount lights on a shelf unit with adjustable shelves; that way you can move the light up and down as needed. Sown trays placed on top of a shelf where the light tube is attached get heat from underneath and the trays and boxes below get the light—it's the perfect deal.

All electrical installations must be grounded and connected to a circuit breaker. In up-to-code electrical panels there is usually a common circuit breaker, in addition to a separate circuit dedicated to the greenhouse. Outlets and cords must be approved for use in humid spaces.

## Heat from lights

All lamps give off heat, which is why plants stretch towards them. If you're going to use lights during the winter, it's a good idea to take advantage of that radiant heat. Lights can be used in the area separated from the rest by insulating plastic bubble wrap. Or make loose plastic tents and hang the lighting inside, but be aware of the fire risk and don't place the lighting lights too close to the plastic.

## Technical installations

Water and electricity are laid out and finished during the greenhouse construction. To be safe, electrical circuits are only to be installed by a qualified electrician. Electricity is needed for lighting and heating; if you enjoy the sound of a water fountain in a mini-pond barrel, remember that this will require electrical work, too.

All outside electrical connections must be grounded and connected to a trip/circuit breaker. You can install low-voltage lighting, pumps and the like (which are connected to a transformer) by yourself without any trouble, as long as they're made for outside use.

*Lanterns and candles are enough to make evenings cozy in the greenhouse.*

# CARING FOR THE GREENHOUSE

A greenhouse needs care and looking after, just like any other building. Tidying and cleaning are integral and necessary steps of caretaking. Cultivation only becomes more difficult if you neglect these tasks, and it increases the likelihood of pests and diseases gaining a foothold.

The greenhouse needs to be cleaned, partly to let in more light during the darker seasons, but also to keep pests and diseases at bay. Insects tend to collect in nooks and crannies—they lay eggs, which then turn into pupae that emerge the following year. Diseases may lurk in the soil, so it needs to be changed out each year.

A greenhouse with an aluminum frame is easy to keep clean, but it should still be rinsed down every so often. A wooden frame requires the same maintenance as any other wooden exterior, including sanding and painting at even intervals. No matter what material the frame is constructed with, the greenhouse's cover material has to be kept clean; dirt, bird droppings, plant debris, soot, and miscellaneous particles landing on the greenhouse need to be washed off. This can be done any time, and preferably several times a year. Most important, though, is to make sure that the greenhouse is clean in the early spring and fall.

## Fall cleaning

Fall cleaning is the biggest chore of the year, and one of the few 'musts' of caring for the greenhouse. Whether you start working on the interior or the exterior first, however, is up to you.

## Exterior

Most greenhouses have some type of drain or gutter along the roof's edge. Start by cleaning this out by hand; you can also pressure wash it with a hose. Check that the rubber edging (if there is one) doesn't come loose. When the gutter is empty of debris, you can give the whole greenhouse a good rinse. A excellent tool for this job is a pressure washer, but use it carefully, as it can put undue pressure on the glass panes. It's often enough to simply give the glass or plastic a thorough rinse.

The lower part of the wall that's nearest the ground often gets very dirty, even on the outside. To limit the spattering of soil along this area, it's a good idea to place stone slabs or gravel along the perimeter when you're building the greenhouse. This lower part is also the most shaded and dampest part of the structure, which makes it an ideal environment for mold and moss to thrive; rinse them off and then scrub the wall with a brush or a sponge, and rinse again. Repeat these steps several times—the moss comes loose pretty easily when it gets wet. There are special products to deal with moss and mold removal.

Once the greenhouse is thoroughly cleaned, it's time to check the condition of the weather strips and clamps holding the glass panes in place; this is done so they stay fastened securely and fit tightly. Gaps that leach in cold air are difficult to fix once temperatures go below freezing, and weather strips around the door are especially vulnerable to wear and tear. Remove sand and debris from doorjambs and tracks. Depending on your greenhouse, it might be necessary to grease the hinges or use silicon spray to make the door open and close more easily. Check also around the base and foundation of the building to ensure no gaps or dents let water seep in or pool inside while the greenhouse is being hosed off.

## Interior

Cleaning starts by removing everything that can be shifted out of the greenhouse. First to go outside: the plants to be saved in addition those to be disposed of. Pots, worktables and furniture are next, tools too. Bring out the window openers from winter storage, as well as strings, ropes, and clips, and throw away any plant debris. Immerse drip irrigation systems, hoses, and drip points in a large bucket filled with warm cleaning water.

Place strings and ropes and clips in hot water. Rinse and change the water several times, always using hot water to kill pests that might have sneaked onto the clips; they won't survive the hot water. Rinse your drip and soaker hoses the same way several times to loosen dirt, soil, and soil particles. If the water is hard and limy, soak the hoses in a citric acid solution to loosen mineral deposits. After soaking, rinse the hoses several times with clean water.

In the spring, recheck all the hoses and drip points before attaching the drip irrigation system. Blow through them to make sure there are no clogs. Until then, keep them, along with the window openers, stored under cover in a frost-free spot—preferably inside.

*Plants are not the only things that thrive in the greenhouse.*

*Fall cleaning in the greenhouse starts with the removal of all wilted plants.*

*Hoses, drip irrigation, and fertilizer containers should be cleaned and then stored in a frost-free area.*

## Houseplants

All your plants need to be taken outside the greenhouse to be rinsed off. Be extra careful to spray underneath the pots and on the underside of leaves. All diseased plants—unless extremely rare or truly special—should to be discarded. Otherwise you run the risk of spreading the disease throughout the greenhouse, in which case you'll have to discard all the plants. Once the plants are rinsed, treat them with horticultural pesticides, if needed, and leave them outside for a while in a sheltered area. You can place diseased plants in a warmer spot to make an infestation run its course, and then run another treatment.

Plants that are going to overwinter should not be potted up until in spring. There's no point in adding new nutrient-rich soil when the plants go dormant through the winter.

Annual plants in pots are to be emptied, soil and all, onto the compost pile. Don't save the soil in the pots for next year's plantings. The soil is nutrient poor and compacted and doesn't reach up to the top of the pot any longer. The plants have consumed the soil, so they need to be potted in new soil in the spring. Don't just add new soil on top of old soil. That's not enough to give the plant a favorable start.

All spent soil that ends up in the compost bin is reusable, but not right away. It needs to be refreshed over a period of time; if left for six months and mixed with other composted materials, it'll be much healthier and can then be used in beds and borders.

Wash the empty pots out, preferably in hot water. Check carefully for slugs, especially at the bottom of the pot where they like to set up house. Leave the pots outside to dry until the greenhouse is clean and ready for them to come back in.

*Change the ground soil and/or add soil from the compost pile.*

*It's important that the glass panes are clean so they let in as much light as possible.*

## The ground soil

Unlike other dirt, the soil in the ground of the greenhouse needs to be replaced as early as fall. The earth you remove can be recycled in the vegetable patch, the compost pile, or used to cover roses and to fill in around bushes and in beds. While there is nothing inherently wrong with the soil used for tomatoes and cucumbers, it's best not to grow the same vegetables in the same soil in consecutive years, as pests that feast on tomato and cucumber plants might overwinter and attack the new plants in the spring. For this reason it's better to refresh at least some of the soil each spring.

You can fill up with a good amount of composted soil in the fall if you like, but not until the fall clean up chores have been seen to. Compost is beneficial and keeps the soil healthy; it even contains nutrients. You don't have to pass the soil through a sieve if there are some larger pieces in it. If composted soil is added in the fall, those chunks will have enough time to decay before

spring. Plus, if you add a 10 cm (4") layer of commercial bagged soil on top, you'll avoid a lot of weeds.

Composted soil is good for the plants and minimizes the risk of disease, but it carries one big disadvantage: it might contain slugs. Slugs feel right at home in compost since they live on plant debris. Check carefully for and kill all slugs immediately, and spread slug bait (the Swedish product called Snaileffect, for example) in the greenhouse once clean-up is complete.

## Scrub and rinse

Once the ground soil is dug out and all the pots are emptied, it's the time for scrubbing and rinsing. Wash, by working from the top down, all the edges, joints, nooks, and crannies; all corners must be rinsed very thoroughly. This will get rid of all insect eggs, pupae and larvae, as well as overwintering insects, fungal spores and the like. If the glass panes are very dirty, use a glass cleaning solution

*The thermometer is an important tool year round. If it is not too cold, it is often too warm.*

or meth spirits after scrubbing them with soft soap and a bristle brush, although try not to let too much cleaning product drip into the ground soil. Soft soap is excellent for scrubbing frames and wooden surfaces. Rinse the paths well, and leave the greenhouse to dry. It's better to take care of this task on a sunny day to give the greenhouse a proper chance to dry out.

## Seal and overwinter

After this thorough cleaning, it's time to move the plants you're keeping back into the greenhouse, and to fill in ground soil. If the greenhouse is fit for winter use, your work is done after cleaning. Plastic bubble wrap is then used to fill in edges, nooks, and crannies. You can also make freestanding plastic tents, bubble wrap

tents or tents from rigid plastic sheets. Before the winter cold sets in, make sure there's a fan heater in place as well as adequate lighting. The thermometer should be in its place, and be visible.

Potted plants that are to be overwintered are moved back inside and placed together for protection. Some plants can be dug down into the ground and then covered with leaves. Other plants might fare better if packed up in pots or boxes with polystyrene, and then covered with burlap. Others are placed close together and then wrapped in shade fabric; it all depends on the plants' individual needs. Everything that is moved inside must be as clean as possible, and the soil in the pots should be slightly humid, but not wet.

## Winter snow

The greenhouse remains mostly dormant during the winter. Plants that are overwintering should be checked at regular intervals, and temperatures should be noted. If it snows, it's OK to leave the snow as an insulating layer; however, the greenhouse roof is usually steep enough so the snow simply slides off. Just keep an eye on things— it's best to sweep the snow off the greenhouse if the weather turns warmer. If the temperature rises suddenly, the snow melts and becomes wet and heavy; if left as is, it will freeze if it gets cold again, and the weight of the ice might make the glass crack. What's more, it's a good thing to shovel or brush the snow up against the sides of the greenhouse, where this added layer provides extra insulation and protection for the plants inside.

## Spring sun

Once the spring sun reappears, it's very important to check the thermometer and the plants. If potted, non-hardy plants have overwintered, they might begin budding green, at which point the soil needs to be humid. When warmer temperatures become more common and it's time to start cultivating, we'll need to start the season with a little sprucing up.

Clean the windows if needed, brush away cobwebs and insects, remove plant debris and wilted leaves, and make sure the place is clean and tidy. Inspect plants closely for pests like aphids, since all small nooks and crannies are potential hiding places for pests.

Install the window openers when the danger of night frost has passed. Until then, keep an eye on things if you have plants in the greenhouse. Temperatures can reach 30°C to 40°C (86°F to 104°F) very quickly on a sunny, late winter's day, and that's not good for the plants. Open the window vents manually during the hottest hours of the day, but close them as soon as the temperature starts dropping again in the afternoon. Soon a new growing season will be in full flower.

# WINTER IN THE GARDEN

## RECOMMENDED READING MATERIAL

Winter is a favorite time for gardeners to peruse seed catalogs, read books and generally to delve deeper into horticultural knowledge.

**To sow rarer plants**

Jekka McVicar, *Seeds: The Ultimate Guide to Growing Successfully from Seeds*, Kyle Cathie 2001
Leo Jelitto m fl, *Hardy Herbaceous Perennials*, Timber Press 1990

**Older volumes**

I also recommend some older books on greenhouse cultivation. Instructional materials for nursery gardens and textbooks on hotbed gardening from a century ago might be found at booksellers dealing in vintage books. These volumes are founts of forgotten knowledge that, while of little use to commercial growers, can still serve the hobby gardener very well—especially with advice on propagation and overwintering. However, they need to be quite old, since books from the 1950s and after tend to champion the use of chemical pesticides, some of which are banned from use today.

## Shopping tips

**Greenhouses and accessories**

The advent of the Internet has changed the ways in which we acquire information as well as how we shop. In Sweden, two large companies, Classicum and Willab, sell greenhouses and their attendant accessories. Both have been in business for many years, are well stocked, and have their own websites. There are also smaller companies that sell their own models, or act as intermediaries for other greenhouse manufacturers. Building supply and discount stores also sell greenhouses, which are usually a special-order item.

Websites:
http://www.classicum.se
http://www.willabgarden.se

The specific insulation fabric used by commercial growers is manufactured by Ludvig Svensson, but is sold through BMS in Hässelholm, Sweden (Telephone: 011- 46- 451 - 38 - 48 - 50). They sell also to the public

(see further information at www.bms.nu).

**Seeds, plants, pots, containers, et cetera.**

Only a few seeds and plants are mentioned by name in this book, because specimen availability tends to change quickly. One of the advantages of having a greenhouse, however, is that it gives us ample opportunity to try out new varieties of seeds and plants.

You can find seeds for growing plants in greenhouses at many horticultural companies, and they're widely available over the Internet. In fact, there are so many retailers that there isn't room to name them all. However, for vegetable seeds, names that stand out are Lindbloms Frö and Runåbergs Fröer. They don't have a brick-and-mortar presence; everything is taken care of by mail order. They and other Swedish outfits have large seed selections to choose from, and their product is of premium quality. Lindbloms Frö also sells seed starting supplies and pots, as well as a variety of items geared specifically to commercial growers.

Impecta Handels is a mail order business selling seeds not only for vegetables and flowers, but also for many kinds of houseplants. Jelitto is a well-known German seed vendor specializing in perennials. They provide excellent seed and sowing information on their website.

Buying plants by mail order can sometimes feel confusing and a bit risky, especially if you're not familiar with the seller and the shipping time is long. There are plenty of reliable vendors, however, and one of them, Rockdala, offers a large selection of their own Swedish grown geraniums and fuchsias.

Websites:
http://www.lindbloms.se/
http://www.runabergsfroer.se
http://impecta.se
http://www.jelitto.com
http://www.rockdala.com/

## THANK YOUS

Many heartfelt thanks to all of you who kindly opened your garden gates and greenhouse doors to me. I am very grateful for the permission you granted me to use photos of your beautiful greenhouses in the pages of this book—an especially big thank you goes to my neighbors on the Swedish island of Hven.

Annica Ahrén and Jan Hansson, Hven
Sten Andersson, Hven
Elna Be, Samlat & Skapat, Förslöv
Ingrid and Arne Bengtsson, Hven
Siv Bengtsson, Vitaby
Else Bratberg, Solna
Citadellets koloniområde, Karlskrona
Marika Csiger-Axelson, Höganäs
Karin Eldforsen, Landskrona
Fredriksdals koloniområden, Helsingborg
Börje Grönhult, Ängelholm
Inge-Mo and Per Gylling, Glumslöv
Maj-Lis and Bosse Hansson, Hven
Maria and Jan-Ingvar Hermansson, Hven
Ulla Hägerlöf, Helsingborg
Ingla Blommor, Billeberga
Sven Johansson, Söderbärke
Kabbarps Trädgård, Åkarp
Margit and Arne Kastberg, Varberg
Larvi Koloniområde, Landskrona
Barbro and Nils Molin, Hven
Christel Roos, Pilehaven Domsten
Eva Tapper and Tommy Svensson, Hven
Trädgårdbutik Viola, Påarp
Tunabergskolonin, Uppsala

# SOURCE AND MATERIALS INDEX

Page references in *italics* indicate a *picture* or a *caption*. **Boldface** indicates more detailed descriptions.

## Plant Index

*Miscellaneous other plants, see lists on pages 44, 46, 48, 52, 60, 84, 95, 115, 126, 127*